ISBN:9798357187574

Rick Paar

God Bless America and Breakfast Burritos to Go

By Rick Paar

For Henry and Marge

Contents

Four Thousand Greyhounds
and Jackie the Leprechaun

God Bless America
and Breakfast Burritos to Go

Nick Takes the Wheel

Four Thousand Greyhounds
and Jackie the Leprechaun

Friday October 11, 2002

From Springfield, Massachusetts to Dewey Beach, Delaware, Susan and I try not to talk about her dog. They have never been apart and she misses him terribly. My two kids are back home taking care of our dog Whitey and I miss them too, but apparently not as much as Susan misses Andre. This is the first time she and I have traveled alone together, I am happy and she is not. I cannot understand her.

Sometimes I think Susan really believes God chose her to mother a being from another species. "I'm driving down the interstate and I see something move and there he is, this fully grown teensy miniature Doberman Pincer all bloody and broken. I could have been looking someplace else but I wasn't. It was like I was meant to find him. Really, Rick, how else would you explain it?"

How else would I explain it? Differently for sure. Luck? Bad luck? But there are certain things you just can't say to a person you think you're in love with, so I have kept my mouth shut.

And here we are, rolling into a small beach town where I have spent vacations with my kids, hoping we can find a nice place for the coming summer and all at once, we are intruders at some kind of annual festival. We are surrounded by hundreds, maybe even thousands, of greyhounds and the people who have adopted them.

Susan is reminded of Andre every time she sees one of these ugly dogs. So am I. I would say this is also bad luck.

Sunday October 13, 2002

We have driven for almost eight hours. The traffic sucks. New Jersey sucks magnificently. The George Washington Bridge and the stupidly named Cross Bronx Expressway suck even more. Susan and I have spoken no more than eight words all day. I am not liking her and she is not liking me. I do not understand the love, the adoration, Susan has for her eight-inch tall shit of a dog who snaps at my ankles, bites my fingers when I try to feed him, and awakens me in the morning snarling at my testicles.

Thursday November 7, 2002

Susan and I limp along for nearly a month before we officially end it at a small Italian restaurant two blocks from her house in Providence on Hope Street.

As big as he is, Andre is not our only problem, of course, but I do blame him and I suppose I do blame her. For the life of me I do not get this devotion, this giving your life over to a dog. Someday I want to understand. Maybe in a year or two. Not tonight. I think tonight I'll have a drink and go to bed.

Two Years Later
Wednesday October 6, 2004 Day One

Three women and their six dogs, all greyhounds, stand on the
sidewalk along Dewey's Main Street, Highway 1. One of the
women says, "I told my husband, you're just gonna have to get
used to them, that's all." The other women nod as one, "That's
right."

The little town is deserted. Some hotels are open. Bars and
restaurants are mostly closed.

Thursday October 7, 2004 Day Two

The streets are filling up with people walking dogs on leashes.
Minivans and SUVs, one after the other after the other, file slowly
into town, most have greyhound decals and bumper stickers,
some have hand painted signs on windows and door panels—
Dewey or Bust! The tenth annual Greyhounds Reach the Beach
celebration has begun and four thousand greyhounds and their
people are here to squeeze one last long weekend out of Dewey
Beach, Delaware.

No Vacancy signs light up. Bars begin to open. The smell of beef
and bacon grease breezes out from packed restaurants.

I follow hand painted signs to a garage bay under a condo unit where a woman has rented retail space for the long weekend. The small area is wall to wall, floor to ceiling, packed with everything greyhound: greyhound Christmas ornaments, greyhound butter dishes, greyhound flags, greyhound cups and mugs (*Can't wait for the caffeine to kick in* on one side *and Whoops, there it is* on the other), greyhound towel holders, greyhound pen holders, greyhound art deco planters, greyhound clothing (primarily snoods and elegant British capes), greyhound key chains, and custom painted denim jackets for the greyhound owner; a steal at $150.

One man who adopts greyhounds talks to another man who also does, "I'd never pay for a dog again." The first man tells the second that he and his wife are here for the whole week at $125 a night. They have four greyhounds and have just bought twenty special greyhound collars at $25 a piece. Each dog has a full wardrobe of coats and snoods and sweaters (ranging in price from $10 to $50) that they wear when the weather gets nippy; anything cooler than a San Diego summer is nippy. The man says his small SUV was big enough when he and his wife owned one greyhound but it felt cramped when they got their second one. They bought a bigger SUV when they got their third. They adopted a fourth greyhound a few months ago and bought a Lincoln Navigator. Lately he's been thinking about getting more dogs and a Hummer.

Free dogs? Crack addicts and golfers spend less.

I step off the sidewalk and into the bike lane of the highway to let seven greyhounds and their two humans walk past. Hounds are everywhere. Here a hound, there a hound, everywhere a hound-hound. I look at the dogs and the people and then I stare straight up at the vertical sights like I'm a tourist on his first trip to New York City and see that every other balcony railing in every hotel is draped with signs advertising wares sold from rooms. Classic K9 Gifts. Greyt Trinkets. Greyt T shirts.

This is now the second time I've experienced anything like this, being surrounded by something so completely alien and still standing on planet earth and I cannot help myself, I spin circles in the street like Mary Tyler Moore in the opening scene from her old sitcom, only she was smiling and I am not.

Friday October 8, 2004 Day Three

I open my hotel room door and stop dead. Seventeen greyhounds waiting for manicures in a room at the end of the hall are lined up, unmoving, snout to rump. It is as quiet as a chemotherapy treatment unit. Each bony dog has a faraway gaze of a starving child waiting to die. I creep down the hall with my back to the wall staring all the way.

It is nearly eighty degrees, the sun is brilliant and the sky is a soft, clear blue and on the street below many people stroll by. Hundreds and hundreds of dogs are on leashes. Dogs and people walk in and out of shops, the people stop to talk to each other while the dogs stand perfectly still. Men and women give great bear hugs to friends they only see once a year here in Dewey. Except for the dogs this could be any group of people at any kind of convention. Yes, except for the dogs. So many dogs.

A blonde woman dressed in long flowing black silk, think a young Stevie Nicks, holds a baby greyhound to her chest as she walks and she twirls a matching black umbrella on her shoulder. A deeply tanned middle-aged couple who look as if they came straight from the golf course, sashay two greyhounds wrapped in pink and black feather boas tied around their necks. They look like dog-street-walkers.

In a screened-in wooden gazebo by the bay, a woman gives psychic dog readings. She will do this for the next few days. She gets forty dollars for a twenty-minute session and is completely booked.

Outside on the street, next to the gazebo, her most recent customer says to a friend, "The psychic lady said it was bur-sitis."

"Not arth-er-ritis?"

"No, she's sure it's bur-sitis."

There is a momentary break in the stream of people coming and going and I duck in to see if the psychic will talk with me for a minute or two about what exactly she does. The woman is about my age and is mortally serious. She and I make no connection. I am escorted out.

I leave the gazebo and take a seat on a park bench overlooking the bay and wait for my next opportunity in twenty minutes. The psychic's assistant, a happy looking woman perhaps seventy, comes out and talks with me for a few moments. With a wide and friendly face, she tells me many stories of her boss's psychic power: How a dog once told the lady in the gazebo about a doughnut it had eaten. How another dog's gas problem turned out to be spirits released from stolen hot dogs and cheese. And how when the psychic was a little girl, a dog warned her of a nearby snake, "Not safe, not safe," the animal whispered. The helper holds a magazine that has a feature article on the woman with the special powers. It is quite impressive, shiny pages and many of them. The assistant tells me that her boss is a "clear-buoyant." I am aware that for the first time in three days I'm smiling.

A tiny old couple has just left the psychic. A bruise colored birthmark covers the left side of the man's badly shaved face and neck. The man's wife walks two steps ahead, an ancient greyhound on a leash limps alongside the man and we all walk together for a while.

"What's her name?" I ask.

"Ruby Suzie," he answers and for the umpteenth time a greyhound name sounds like a stripper.

"She's a pretty old dog," I say.

"Got an older one back home. He couldn't make the trip."

"So, you have two dogs?"

The woman turns around and says, "We only got two greyhounds but we got more'n two dogs." She lifts the front pockets on her vest, first her left one then her right one, and bares two tiny dogs nestled comfortably above her breasts.

"So, you have four dogs?"

"Oh, we have more'n four," she says and turns her back to me again. "Take a look."

I peek inside her backpack and see two more small dogs.

"Six? You have six dogs?"

"Oh, my. We have more'n that. Show him the picture," the man says and in a second I am being handed a Christmas card photo that includes these two people, these five dogs and ten other dogs.

I begin to count. "There's fifteen," she says.

I am smiling again and I am speechless and my eyes are welded to the picture. I ask if she can name them all, and she begins, pointing at each, telling me its name and occasionally telling a quick story about its personality.

"What's your family think of having fifteen dogs?"

"Oh, dear, they are our family."

Finally, I say to the old man, "If you don't mind my asking, why did you see the psychic?"

"We wanted to see if Suzie was happy with us."

"Is she?"

"Yes. I believe she is."

Across the highway on an Astroturf covered deck that sits on top of the Beach Fries Grille, two women are sitting on white plastic chairs at a white plastic table. One woman is very large and has two tiger-striped greyhounds at her feet. (I will learn later that tiger-striped greyhounds are called brindles.) The other woman is on the short side, stocky with mid-length bleached blonde hair, looks to be near fifty, but she might be younger. This second woman will work from noon to five through Saturday afternoon, and just like her counterpart on the bayside, she is also booked solid every twenty minutes. The weekend schedule of activities lists her program title, "What is My Greyhound Trying to Tell Me?" She is a Licensed Clinical Social Worker. She too is a psychic.

Her client has just left and there doesn't appear to be another one waiting at the moment so I walk over and ask if we can talk until her next appointment arrives. She smiles and agrees but says she needs a moment or two to collect herself. While I wait, she waves her hands at the air above her head the way someone might grab at a cobweb in dim light.

I ask her what she does with the dogs.

"I communicate with them."

"How do you do that?" I ask.

She looks unblinking into my eyes and she smiles again. "The spirits. The angels. They tell me."

There is a deep intensity to this woman and she is as serious about her craft as her unlicensed competitor across the street, but this woman is an awful lot easier to talk with. She tells me that her mom died when she was four years old and she began to feel this frightening new power. "It was like the floodgates opened. There was constant chatter. The spirits didn't stop talking to me," she says. It scared her and when she tells me this I can really feel just how frightened and alone that little girl must have been.

"I never told anyone about the voices. When I was a teenager a therapist helped me. She told me I had the gift."

"Are the spirits and angels always with you?" I ask, and she says that they are.

"So, how do you control them?"

"I just tell them, 'Hey, I'm a human being, you know, and I'm not working right now so come back later, OK?' And if that doesn't work I wave them away." Which, I guess, explains the cobwebs.

On the way down the stairs I pass a man with a smallish greyhound who is next in line.

Later in the day, outside of the greyhound-Reiki workshop, I see the man with the smallish greyhound again. I ask him why he saw the Psychic Social Worker.

"Jason's having trouble adjusting to our family and I wanted to see how he was feeling."

Jason is from Spain, a Galgo greyhound who never raced. "He was kept in a pen like it was Auschwitz," the man growls. Apparently, there were a hundred dogs, many very aggressive, and when food was tossed into the middle of the tight pack a steel-caged death match ensued, a cross between Darwin and the WWE. Some dogs ate well and grew fat and others shrank and died. The man adopted Jason last summer, skinny but alive.

The man is no fan of the Spanish. "Do you know what they do for good luck? They hang a dead greyhound by the neck from a tree ..."

Or something like that, I'm not sure what he is saying, because I'm still stuck on the image of a hundred dogs fighting for food which makes me think about what another man told me this morning, greyhounds being piled up dead—fifty at a time—in the back of a pickup being driven from the track to a pit. And the next thing I know my brain has wandered off to my friend Joe, and his father's life as a kid in a Nazi labor camp, slashed with a bayonet, beaten but alive, unlike his family all murdered and dumped on a pile of other dead people like they were shit-stained laundry.

What the hell is it with humans?

I am pulled back from my drift when the man says, "... maybe it can help Jason."

"What can?"

"Reiki. I had it done to me a few year ago and it felt pretty good."

"Has any of this stuff worked? The psychic, the massages?" I ask.

"I don't know yet." But the man seems to have faith that it will. He seems to have faith particularly in the Social Worker because "She told me something that no one else could have ever known."

"What's that?"

"She told me that Jason has an eating disorder," and I am shocked, shocked, as Claude Rains said in Casablanca.

"But, she was wrong about our other dog," he says quietly. "She said that our other greyhound has ADD but she's a real lazy bones. A total couch potato."

I see two greyhound puppies prance by. These are the second and third greyhound puppies I've seen, the first being the one held by the Stevie Nicks woman in black silk. They are frisky and even kind of cute which is very much different from the adult greyhounds who move slowly and look more concocted than born; kind of like mother nature had gone home after a hard night of drinking gin, grabbed a bunch of leftover animal parts from the freezer—a pointy rat nose, skinny deer legs, a lizard tail—grafted them all to a massive set of lungs and then passed out before she could find the body fat and fur. Greyhounds are not pleasing to look at. And, even more, truly every single greyhound I have seen is in some way scarred: all shapes, all sizes, all over. Some scars are pinpricks, some are long and razor thin, some are jagged and wide and some are like Morse code. I am told that all greyhounds have skin like old parchment paper, very thin and very fragile, so when they race and are run over by a faster hound, or scrape against the fence or snag themselves on a wire, they bleed and scab.

Seeing greyhound puppies feels weirdly good, like a new generation is growing up outside of the dog-track and won't have to live with cuts and bruises. They can just be dogs. Maybe they'll do dog things like barking or fetching or humping a leg instead of sitting quiet like they're in a Tennessee Williams play, deep in the south, deep in the heat, dozing on the porch, nowhere to go.

I talk with someone who has a greyhound puppy and discover that it isn't a greyhound puppy at all. The little thing, and it is little, is an Italian Greyhound. They are known as IG's but everyone calls them Iggy's for short. I am more than a little bit bummed that there are no puppies.

Before I fall asleep for the night I think about this adoption thing, about how a person can take in another being and completely commit. I think about how both lives can never be the same, how, when it works, each gives life over to the other. How, when it doesn't work it resembles a hostage situation.

I used to teach psychology at a small state college in the Nebraska with a woman whose husband decided to run for the state senate. We all thought that was very cool and, son of a gun, he won. They already had a twelve-year old blonde-haired, blue-eyed daughter but soon after the victory they decided to adopt a blonde-haired, blue-eyed, seven-year old girl named Ramona. The two girls looked like blood-sisters and after Ramona was washed and cleaned the four of them made for one terrifically photogenic family.

Ramona was bought new clothes, fed good food and at night had good books read to her. *The Just Right Family* was her favorite. Ramona's name was changed to something that sounded less swarthy, less exotic, something like Jennifer or Melissa. I forget exactly which.

Campaign-family holiday photos were sent to constituents, "We Wish You and Yours the Merriest Christmas Ever" and they all looked perfect. Two handsome parents and two beautiful daughters.

Ramona was a tough child. She had been abandoned by her mother and shuttled from foster home to foster home and never quite figured out how to be with people. Sometimes she was too loud, sometimes too quiet and withdrawn, but always she never really fit in. She probably stole things and broke things and did other stuff, too. Lord knows she had been hurt in her previous life and it showed. She must have been hard to live with. But, you know, you make a commitment, right?

One day I heard someone ask the new state senator, "What are you getting Ramona for Christmas?"

"Luggage," he said.

And in a matter of weeks, Ramona or Melissa or Jennifer or whatever they were calling her at that point, snuggled in with her new-mother one night and was told, "Do you remember that book I used to read to you? *The Just Right Family*?"

"Yes, mommy."

"Well not all families are just right, you know. So tomorrow we're going to have to take you back. G'night, honey."

Saturday October 9, 2004 Day Four

Finally, everyone is here, four thousand greyhounds and not quite as many people. It's a Hitchcock movie but with dogs. Today is The Blessing of the Hounds. I have circled and re-circled it on my schedule. It will begin at ten thirty and I have no idea what happens but everyone has told me it is beautiful and I cannot miss it.

At twenty past ten the crowd slips as a single cell toward the beach at the end of Read Street. I wander through the assembly, possibly a thousand or more dogs and a few less people, and all are dead quiet. I find a spot in the middle of it all. A small stage sits at the base of the seawall, just beneath a flamingo-pink eight-story hotel. Two Black women in maid uniforms stand on a third-floor balcony and gaze down on all of us white people and these well-dressed dogs. I will see only three other Black people here this weekend, an off-duty housekeeper and two men in a convenience store.

One little girl wearing Mouseketeer ears stands with her parents near me. I have seen no more than a few dozen children since

Wednesday. I am so surprised that I take their picture. The service begins.

A priest and minister alternate speaking for the next fifteen minutes, one small voice then the other. They read soft and touching prayers, a passage from the Book of Job, a Native American Blessing, a prayer from St. Francis:

> *Blessed are you, Lord God, maker of all living creatures. You called forth fish in the sea, birds in the air and animals on the land ...*

I look out over the ocean. Gulls kamikaze into the sea and return to the surface with small fish in their mouths. Over and over again they dive. And, filled, suddenly, quietly, they fly away as one.

Dolphins swim in the gentle swells out past the small coil of breaking waves, gliding under water, arcing for a moment and then gliding again. A man swims with the dolphins, also beyond the wave-break, but closer to shore: slower, fitful and plodding, but graceful for a man. Behind me, I hear a prayer from Albert Schweitzer:

> *Hear our humble prayer, O God, for our friends the animals, especially for animals who are suffering; for any that are hunted or lost or deserted or frightened or hungry; for all that must be put to death. We entreat for them all Thy mercy and pity,*

and for those who deal with them we ask a heart
of compassion and gentle hands and kindly words.
Make us, ourselves, to be true friends to animals
and so to share the blessings of the merciful ...

I turn around when I hear the priest ask us to remember our old pets. "Remember their names. Remember how they felt when you held them. Remember how they cared for you when you were sick. Remember how you cared for them. Say their names. Say them out loud."

I can't believe I follow his instruction, but I do. I say, "Pepper, Pepper Two, Sauerkraut, Whitey." My throat burns. My voice catches. My eyes tear. I wipe my nose.

All around me men and women, also wiping tears and sniffing, begin to speak, "Bunny, Togo, Lips, Arnold, Killer, Mr. President ..." I see the priest begin to cry as he recites the names of his old dogs, too.

And, in a few seconds, everything is still again and dogs in the sand sit bored.

I turn to the ocean. The birds have flown off, the dolphins and the swimming man are long gone, too.

From the silence, a guy in the crowd howls like a wolf, and as if it were a tap of a baton on a music stand, every dog cocks its head,

RCA Victor style, and lets out a howl that, all together creates its own crazy chorus of HOWL!!!HOWL!!!HOWL!!!

For the next two minutes this sound washes me, tickles me, and I'm a little kid again. I take the mini tape recorder out of my pocket and hold it high above my head to record this sound I've never before heard and will hear again only if I return to Dewey.

In the evening, around eight o'clock, I drop by the Bottle and Cork bar to see the Beer and Biscuits Ball where greyhounds are dressed up like ballplayers and bankers, cowboys and cops, astronauts and sailors, hookers and hoods, kings and queens and of course the Village People. "Oh, you missed the best ones," I am told.

Parked along the street next to the Bottle and Cork is a large van with a professionally done sign on its side — *The Greyhound Gang.* The woman who owns the van is about my age and asks if I can help her move some boxes. She is gently and persistently persuasive and as I begin to hoist the boxes, people stop to talk with her as if she were a kind of celebrity. They all want to be close to her but are respectful of the greyhound royalty that she is. "How was your trip? It's such a long way. Oh, I wish I could do what you do," they say.

A few years ago, Claudia gave up a big, high-paying job in New York City to move to Kanab, Utah to rescue greyhounds three dozen at a time. I am open-mouthed when she tells me this.

"Three dozen? Jesus, why?"

"It's a long story but basically I loved the greyhound I had and was getting tired of my job and wanted to do something that made me happy. Something that made a difference. I was getting near fifty, you know?"

Yes, I know. Four years ago, I turned fifty. I get it. The joints that begin to ache for no reason, the friends who have died, the memories of times you'll never have again, the stupid things you've done, the loves you've had, the loves you've lost, the wish that you could screw up the nerve to bag this entire mess of a career and blast off to parts unknown and start over.

And Claudia did it. She actually did it. Someone my age, for whatever reason, said the hell with it and packed up and left. Claudia has become my hero.

We exchange email addresses. "Really, I mean it, send me an email. If you ever find yourself out in Kanab, stop in. I'll show you around."

"Absolutely," I say, but I won't. Kanab? Utah? No one just "finds himself out in Kanab?" If you're ever going to go to Kanab or change your life at fifty you pretty much need to have a plan. I don't think you just pack a big bag and leave.

I say so long to Claudia and stroll back outside into the dark and see the usual thousand dogs on leashes and what made me so oddly startled a couple of days ago has become just one more walk down Main Street, saying hello to most people, nodding a greeting to the rest, moving off the sidewalk to let a pack of animals walk by, and walking with my head down when the sidewalk is my own. I see that most light poles are urine soaked at the base.

And without warning, suddenly I am greyhounded out.

I need to find a place where dogs aren't allowed. A place just for humans.

At the end of the commercial strip, I walk into the Dewey Beach Club where I sit at the mostly empty bar, exactly one seat to the left of where I sat two years ago drinking Guinness with Susan and an old guy named Jackie. It was easily the best part of our trip, probably the only time we laughed.

I'll be damned. Jackie is here, down at the end of the bar, drinking Budweiser from a long-necked bottle, quietly attending to every word a very pretty middle-aged woman is telling him about a wedding she and her husband recently went to. He looks just the way I remembered him: small, almost tiny, old, wrinkled, big smile, thick white hair, thick glasses inside too big-for-his-face black frames.

When the woman leaves, I ask the bartender to send Jackie a Bud but he says that Jackie's had a lot to drink tonight, "How 'bout I give him a chit for tomorrow?" and the bartender tosses the round coaster good for one free beer down to Jackie and points to me when he does. "It's from him," he says.

Jackie lifts the beer he is drinking and salutes me by angling the bottle in my direction and smiling. I leave my seat to talk with him.

"I remember you from two years ago when I was here. How've you been?" I ask.

I know Jackie doesn't remember me although he says he does. He still lives alone in a trailer. Still plays jazz guitar by himself. Still comes to the bar, I'm guessing most nights, and still looks a lot like a leprechaun. "So, what brings you back to Dewey?" he asks.

"The greyhounds."

"You have one?"

"No, I was just curious why people would adopt them."

"They don't hurt no one," Jackie says.

I agree with him, we talk a few minutes more, I say good-bye and walk back to my room.

And as I drift in and out of sleep, I think about Jackie. How Jackie is old and quiet. How he is broken and harmless. How he is alone. And then it hits me. Jackie is not alone. The Dewey Beach club has adopted him. They are his family and Jackie is their greyhound.

I think I got what I came for. Maybe not completely, but at least a little.

Forest Park - Springfield, Massachusetts
Thursday July 14, 2005

I have had four dogs, two of which were named Pepper. The first Pepper was, naturally enough, a Dalmatian. The second Pepper was a Beagle. Our third dog was a mixed-up stew my little sister named Sauerkraut thinking one day it would decide to be a German Shepherd. All three did usual dog things. One or all of them humped legs, sniffed random crotches, bellowed in the woods at three in the morning, ran in the park with my father, and acted like a heating pad when you were sick. One was hit by a motorcycle and lived, another was hit by a car and lived, and one of them lived a double life—three or four days with us, three or four days with a family much like ours who thought they had found a stray. Two were said to have been "given away to a farmer where she'll be happy." Only one actually was, and it wasn't the one whose two favorite things to eat were crayons and, hours later, her own colorful feces.

My present dog is named Whitey. My kids and I got her from the pound a day or two before her short little life would have been snuffed out. She is mid-sized. She is fat. She has long hair that makes her look even fatter. She is all black and she does dog things. She barks. She barks at the coming dark. She barks at the men putting on a new roof next door. She barks at the sound of the mailman. She does wind sprints up and down the stairs, spins cartoon circles on the hardwood floor, and skids on her chest when I open the door to let her out for a run with me and my friend Joe and his dogs Duke and Draco. She farts and has no idea that it was she who farted. (Or maybe she just pretends, I don't know.) She rummages through the trash to find anything with protein still attached; dental floss, old cheese wrappers, and paper towels with bacon grease are three of her favorites. She wants to be let out. No, let in. No, out. In. Out. She sleeps a lot. She loves to be scratched on her haunches; her tongue slides out of her mouth and her eyes roll back. I leave her in the yard when I go to work and at night she snores on the floor next to my bed, not in it because Whitey is a dog.

It has been nearly a year since I was last in Dewey surrounded by greyhounds. I thought about that trip nearly every day for many months, but real-life requires attention to the niggling details of making a living and taking care of kids and in time the memory of large dogs dressed as sailors and street-walkers faded. And then two days ago, on a path in the woods of the large city park where Joe and I have run at least a thousand times before, Whitey, my silly, black, long-haired, fat-pawed, gentle, lick-you-until-you-say-uncle dog, was attacked by two pit bulls who were walking off-leash, ten feet from their owner. I screamed curses at the thugs. Joe screamed, too. Joe's dogs, Whitey's best friends, Duke and Draco, howled in a sympathetic agony. The pit bulls' owner, a woman Joe and I had seen once or twice a week for years, each time quite friendly, begged her dogs to stop, saying loud and surprised, "I can't believe they are doing this." She yanked on their collars, "Please stop. Please," she cried. Again and again I kicked at the dogs' ribs as one dog gnawed its fangs into Whitey's neck and the other did likewise to her haunches; smaller versions of two lions bringing down a water buffalo on an old episode of *Wild Kingdom*.

And then the assassins broke off their ambush with no more warning or reason than it had begun and strolled away, just two blocks of muscle and bone continuing the afternoon leg of their twice daily walk in the park, doing nothing more than what they were bred to do, mauling animals in the wild. Whitey, her tail between her legs, slinked away fast in a Groucho Marx crouch, looking as if she thought this mugging was somehow her fault, that she must have done something to provoke this blindside assault from two animals who, despite being loved and cared for by a lady from a good neighborhood who lived in a good house, had reverted to the instinctual action for which humans had created them many years before.

Later that day a veterinarian pronounced Whitey bloodied and bowed but basically OK. Back home, my kids and I hugged her and kissed her and fed her every dog-treat she wanted until she finally turned up her nose at bacon and cheese.

I don't know exactly why, but somehow those hair-triggered, flesh-ripping, remorse-free pit bulls got me thinking again about the greyhounds; how both were now anachronisms bred by humans for specific tasks utterly pointless in a modern suburban world—clamping down jaws on wild boars in the former, and land speed greater than the game their masters hunted in the latter.

I want to see the greyhounds one more time. This time I need to see what they can do. I need to see them run. So, it's off to a nearby dog track for a week of racing.

A Week at the Dog Track - Hinsdale, New Hampshire
Wednesday August 3, 2005

Hinsdale Greyhound Park is a dry-docked ship, old and white and wooden, anchored at the back end of a cracked and broken asphalt lot that ought to be attached to a Mammoth Shopping Mall in New Jersey. It is many-many-many times larger than it needs to be. Twenty-two cars are parked here this morning.

On the inside, Hinsdale looks like a small-town desert bus station from a black and white movie. The place is scrubbed clean and dull, smelling everywhere, inescapably, but not overpoweringly so, of ammonia which is breathed with every breath and makes it eventually gone. Old giant pivoting fans positioned where people gather blast hot air back and forth, back and forth, back and forth, and it feels just as hot inside, as it does outside where the radio-guy says it's ninety-six degrees.

Two breezy girls, perhaps juniors or seniors in high school, stand behind the laminate and glass counter in the lobby. They are here to sell candy bars, cigarettes, gum, newspapers, and racing forms but most of their time is spent staring down at the ads in flipped-open, unsold magazines. They giggle together about the hot boys and the cool clothes they see and, when required, they blindly and silently make change for the old people who might as well be their estranged grandparents.

I say hello and give them a couple of dollars. They give me a program. No eye contact. No words. They act as if I'm one of the old people.

Around the corner from the blooming girls, the eyes of five old men are fixed like thick-glassed laser beams on distant ponies running inside TV screens bolted high on the wall in the wide hallway between the entrance and the circular bar which, because it is not quite noon, is not yet open. The men wear baseball caps, polyester shorts, discount house sneakers (there's not a Nike swoosh in sight), and T-shirts bought on long ago vacations. They root in quiet. Their lips move hopefully at first, and later in whispered curses when their television horses from someplace much nicer and much farther away finish out of the money. Tickets are ripped and dropped on the tired linoleum floor. "Son of a bitch. Goddamn it. Shit," they mutter.

They are not the lucky ones and they know it. They want to be somewhere else—Saratoga, Delmar, Hialeah—but they are here, in this old broken down bus station of a place where greyhounds leave every ten minutes and travel in small, thirty-second ovals.

On the far side of the bar, just next to the closed sliding glass door that leads to the asphalt patio next to the track, four more old men sit around a lone plastic table. Each man is hunched over today's racing form, each has a cigarette in his hand. No one speaks. No one looks at anyone. They cover their forms the way smart kids in high school cover their multiple-choice tests. Every now and then they sleepwalk to the one open betting window on the far wall.

The sun is big and glowing and seems to be stalled over Vermont just a few hundred yards west of here on the other side of the Connecticut River. Two bare headed old people from inside have moved partway outside into a thin sliver of shade. I take a spot at an empty plastic table on the far right side of the patio down by the rail next to the smooth, dry, dirt track.

Bored kids wearing green polo shirts and tan khaki pants parade bored dogs on leashes up and down the track making sure to pause before us so that we might ...

We might what? What are we supposed to be looking for? How do you tell one greyhound from another? They still look alike to me, the way they did in Dewey. Big and ugly and no personality. But right at this moment, dressed in their racing colors, the dogs are Roman gladiators marching around the Coliseum before the death-matches. Either that or Miss America contestants walking the runway.

An old woman sitting by herself eats hot chili and smokes a cigarette in the miserable heat.

A disembodied male voice on the loudspeaker, bored and torpid and gravelly, begins to speak and I cannot understand a word he says. It sounds, appropriately, like a bus station intercom voice; four in the morning, filled with sleep, not wanting to be here, counting the hours until the new guy arrives.

Two of the kids who paraded the dogs in front of us a few minutes ago hold muzzles in their hands and run down the track as fast as they can. One kid peels off at the finish line in front of me and the other kid, much fatter and extremely sweaty, waddles farther down the track past the first turn. I watch the fat kid until he stops. Then I …

… *JESUS CHRIST THEY ARE FAST* …

When I turn around the greyhounds have already finished the first quarter of the race, moving past the patio and the four of us outside in the fierce sun.

Down at the first turn in a tight NASCAR dog-pack, Number 3 cartwheels in the air and lands on his feet like it was planned and I whisper a little cheer, "Go Number 3, Go!" But Number 2, who has lead from the start is much faster than all the other dogs and his lead gets increasingly large until it gets so large that on the back stretch he begins to look around like he's lonely, like he wants a friend, like he wants some other dog to play with. And while Number 2 pauses, Number 8 on the outside breezes right by—as do three others—and Number 2 finishes fifth, two spots ahead of the acrobatic Number 3.

And everywhere there is silence.

No racing hooves. No snorting. No jockeys going to the whip. And there is absolutely no crowd noise, either. No one cheers. No one makes a sound. This is not a crowd behavior I am familiar with. I am trying to think of a sport where the fans are this quiet.

Golf? Not anymore. Tennis? No. Chess? Yes, chess. Matinee greyhound races sound a lot like chess. Only not as loud.

I hear two guys near me talking and I turn to take a peek. One man is, of course, very old. Nearly everyone is. The other is in his late thirties; small, barely five feet tall and his chin seems to have been swallowed into his neck. In a thick New England accent he talks about incredibly fast, but all too sociable, dog Number 2. "I'd straighten him out in a hurry. I'd take a gun or a bat and BOOM—he wouldn't do that again, that's for sure." He has a weird chuckle when he says this, kind like an old time movie villain. The younger guy keeps talking, angrily moving from animal cruelty to liberal Massachusetts politicians (even though Mitt Romney is our governor). "All those taxes and they can't fix the goddamned roads." I stand up to take a longer look and see that he is a sorry little man who has probably been ignored by everyone except for this old man who is trying hard to ignore him, too, but the little-man holds him by the arm and won't let him leave.

A very large GMC pickup truck with a big water tank smooths the track for the next race and the bus station voice begins. Again, I cannot make out what he says and a couple of tables to my left, the old woman keeps eating hot chili and between plastic spoonsful she fires up yet another cigarette.

All of this happens in the same dark silence as before. And then a weird fart-noise breaks through the still air. I glance over at a man in black sitting alone at the next table. And as I look at him I can see out of the corner of my eye a small white furry object begin whirring very fast around the track from across the oval beneath the pines and at that exact same time the garbled voice says in a growly-singsong, the first four words that I can understand, "Here comes the colonel," and this next race has started and JESUS CHRIST—again—they are fast, wicked fast, I cannot describe just how fast, oh my God they are fast. FAST. They don't look real.

I think the winners are Numbers 1, 3, and 7 but I am not sure and I don't really care because I am still stunned by their SPEED. Today is the first time I've seen a greyhound off-leash and never in my life, with my own naked eyes, have I seen another living thing run this fast.

After a few more races the heavy sunshine begins to burn and the patio has emptied. I finally go inside, too, but continue up the stairs to the not quite enclosed grandstand where threadbare seats, steep pitched aisles and sagging water stained ceilings makes the place look and feel like a balcony in a once plush, long ignored, movie theater from the forties. Partitions surround each small section and once I take my seat I can see the track but no one else in the grandstand and because of that and the constant quiet I feel as if I'm alone.

And then it's more running kids, another rabbit-fart, one more cracked voice, and one more race, and instead of the track below I'm watching a bird that has flown inside the grandstand try to fly back out through one of the open windows. He perches on the sill of the tallest window and looks out toward the track before he takes off. He loops around and around inside the grandstand and comes back to the same spot on the sill.

I root for him. "You can do it. Come on bird. Figure it out."

It takes him three tries to escape.

Thursday August 4, 2005

Once when I was nineteen, on a spring-break-whim, with twenty bucks in my pocket, I hitchhiked to Florida with a friend of mine, Bob MacNeil, a Black guy with hair as tall and frizzed as a bush in an English garden. At the last Howard Johnson's on the Jersey Turnpike (where my grandmother would drop dead nine years later) we got a ride from a Cuban refugee and a kid AWOL from the Air Force. They had a brand new, top of the line fancy Volvo, probably stolen, and Bob and I rode in luxury all the way to Fort Lauderdale beach where we stumbled upon five or six of our friends who had driven south for spring break. On the second night there we all went to the Jai Alai matches and I lost eighteen of my twenty dollars. That was the beginning and end of my gaming life.

I have never understood betting and the sweet old man who was yesterday's audience for the angry little man with no chin is trying to teach me what he knows. He is frustrated because I just don't get it. "There's win …" he says.

 "OK, I got that," I say.

"… and place. That's second …"

"Right, got that one, too."

"… and show. That's the one that comes in third."

And I'm OK so far.

"Then you can key," he says.

"Huh?"

"Or quinella."

"Huh?"

"Or you can box."

This one I know because my grandfather played the number 6-2-5 boxed every day of his life. It was one of the few things he lived for and when cancer swept across his body and took out his larynx and his eyes went blurry from a botched cataract surgery, my grandmother would make the daily trip to the corner store to bet a buck on that incredibly unlucky number which never ever hit. Except, of course, for the one day it did hit which was the one day she didn't buy a ticket. My grandfather, unable to talk, beeped his humming voice-box-wand at her until the battery died.

Largely, I am hopeless with this betting-thing and this man who yesterday put up with the rantings of an idiot is today absolutely incredulous, almost annoyed at me. "It's all right there up on the board," he says shaking his head pitifully. "You really don't know, do you?

No I don't.

I sit at the island bar and watch an inning or two of the Red Sox game. The couple to my right is drinking beer, smoking cigarettes and watching the game, too, but they also glance from TV set to TV set watching a slew of horse races being beamed in from all over the planet. The wife is retired-attractive: intense tan, blue eyes,

TV news anchor blonde hair, wide smile, trim but probably not exactly healthy. She's just north of seventy and her husband, who is maybe five years older, looks just awful, like he's a big drinker with bleary eyes, broken blue veins on his big round nose, and thin red skin on his face and body which leaks a powerful sweat even as he sits still. His shirt is drenched and he can't seem to get comfortable. The man and I make guy-talk about Matt Clement, the Red Sox pitcher who got hit in the head the other day, "Bet you don't remember Herb Score?" the man says. But I do, "Sure, pitched for the Indians in the fifties. Gil McDougal hit him in the eye with a line drive."

"Ruined him. Could have been a Hall of Famer," he says. Turns out, down in Florida, where he and his wife live most of the year, he is a friend of a friend of Herb Score.

It also turns out that the man and his wife own two greyhounds.

"Ever been to Dewey Beach?" I ask thinking that anyone who owns more than one greyhound has at least thought of making the pilgrimage.

"What's Dewey Beach?" asks the woman.

"Three or four thousand rescued greyhounds take over this little beach town in Delaware every Columbus Day Weekend. It's crazy. You really ought to go," I say.

"*Rescued* greyhounds? Our greyhounds race. Cost us fifteen hundred a piece." The man says this with some amount of pride, almost turning up his exploded nose.

I'm a little taken aback, I've never met anyone who owned racing hounds and I want to know more so I quickly rattle off as many questions as I can think of. Why do you own them? Do they live with you? Is it hard to teach them to chase the rabbit? How often do they work out?

But they don't know any more about greyhounds than I do. A trainer takes care of the dogs, feeds them, cleans them, houses them and gets them ready to race. The wife sounds fatigued, "Oh, they're just a hobby."

"Yeah, they give you a little something to root for when you go to the track," says her husband.

Part investment, part entertainment. The dogs are pure commodity. Nothing more. Nobody knows who they are. No one really gives a shit. Greyhounds might just as well be fleshy ping pong balls in a giant lottery machine. Today's winning number, 8-4-5-7-2-1-3-6.

Tonight I go to a bar back home. I tap my feet and clap my hands to Zydeco music, laugh nonstop with my friend Mike-the-writer, and tell him about the past two days watching greyhounds, the old people who bet on them, and the old people who own them.

I have many beers. Too many beers. I want to forget about old things and I do for a while.

Friday August 5, 2005

It's 4:10 AM, I've had too little sleep, too much to drink, my head is thick and I'm walking into my parents' house which smells everywhere of fresh, raw, rank shit that will not go away until days later when the place is scrubbed clean with ammonia.

My mother called a couple of minutes ago and asked if I could come over, "Your father's having a hard time." He is on the toilet at the top of the stairs—door open, his head in his hands, straining, trying to shit, trying to not shit, having no control of his skinny, bony, shaking, sweating, body—mostly he has hit the toilet, but the trail from his bed, my old bed, to the bathroom five steps away suggests that he has sometimes missed.

My father has been visited by a peculiar kind of intestinal blockage for the past few years. It's been diagnosed and misdiagnosed, treated and not, and sometimes it, whatever it is, doesn't bother him and other times it buckles him, beats him up and wrings him out so that he needs to stop everything and rest for a couple days. He has also, in recent years, had an arterial blockage and a carotid artery blockage; the former resulting in cardiac bypass surgery, the latter causing a mini-stroke and, a week later, a Roto-Rootering called a carotid endarterectomy.

There have been little things, too; a double hernia operation, persistent skin problems, hyponatremia (an almost fatal washing away of body salt), and a not-exactly-precise repositioning of his heart after the bypass surgery so that it is literally accurate, but not really true, to say of him that his heart hasn't been in the right place for fifteen years. And then, as desert, seven years ago he was knocked on his ass by a stupid mutant strain of Tuberculosis, Avium Bacterium Intracellular Disease (ABI), which almost always strikes old women or chemotherapy patients or people who are HIV positive, none of which he is. Unlike its cousin, his version of TB has no magic antibiotic to make it all go away so right now his lungs work at about forty percent of what they used to and his world has shrunk down to this house and neighborhood and not-so-long-trips in the car because sometimes the intestinal-thing thinks it is a squadron of bombers and he is Pearl Harbor. But there's good news on the ABI front. His lung doctor assures him that he'll probably die with it but not of it.

And here he sits broken hearted, lived his life and only farted ... and grunted and strained and labored to breathe and is doubled over and I stand next to him petting his head with my hand, putting cool wash rags on his blistered scalp, telling him it'll be all right, telling him that I love him, trying not to cry watching him struggle to take a crap like he was one of my kids twenty years ago on the toilet for the first time.

After a couple of hours he thinks he's OK to go back to bed and does. I lie down on my sister's old bed and try to sleep but don't. I suppose if I'm lucky I'll also live to be eighty. Just like he is.

No Hinsdale, no greyhounds, and no old people I do not know today.

Saturday August 6, 2005

I feel shitty. I feel more than shitty. I feel sad. I feel sad for my father. I do not like seeing him old and sick, living in a shrunken world and moving toward death.

I feel myself getting old, I feel my own life shrinking. I have begun to realize that I am at the front edge of old-age and I can begin to see the end from here. I think I saw it last night on the toilet.

So, all-in-all, I'm not happy about going back for two more days to this sad, old dog-track.

Oh, and today is the sixtieth anniversary of Hiroshima which allowed me to be born because it probably saved my father's life when he was fighting in World War Two in the South Pacific. Yippee.

It's Saturday night and there are a lot more people here than there were a couple of days ago. Old people are still in the majority but tonight they all seem hidden among the couples on dates and families with kids. Most of the not-yet-old-men have leftover mullet haircuts, wear Harley-Davidson (or Red Sox or Dale Earnhardt) "wife beater" shirts, and stand smoking cigarettes in James Dean poses that scream to the world, "DON'T FUCK WITH ME." Their girlfriends and wives (who also do not fuck with them) were probably all cute in high school, but that was about forty-five pounds ago and now they fill out their shorts and shirts like potatoes in bags. Everyone is aging rapidly. Someday they will be hanging on, just getting by, maybe even becoming the matinee old-folks at the OTB TV screen but I don't imagine they are thinking that right now.

At the combination poker lounge, casino, and supposedly upscale restaurant, I eat a lousy dinner—burnt shrimp, not-quite-cooked vegetable ragout—and it's like the chef's just hanging on too, just like everything in this rundown place.

And down below, the truck grooms the track, the kids parade the next group of dogs in front of the stands and suddenly the ritual is broken for a moment when one of the dogs stops to take an enormous dump on the smoothed track. Considering last night's events, I take this as a sign of good luck. He wins the race but I didn't bet.

My smiling waitress asks, "Is everything, OK?"

"Yes," I lie.

I'm back. It's Sunday. Last day. Thank God.

The place is less crowded than last night but more crowded than a weekday afternoon. Some of the people look like they came to the track straight from church which makes a kind of sense. Faith beats Reason by a nose.

Everyone, no matter how they're dressed, looks old and conquered or young and hard, the way people have looked all week, just poor folks getting poorer two-dollars at a time.

The old couple I met Friday, the ones who own two racing greyhounds and live in Florida, are back again today. It turns out they are originally from Springfield, my hometown, and, small-world, the man grew up at the other end of my street. We play the "do you know so and so game" with no more luck than I expected; it was a long street and he's a lot older. Finally, I ask the reflex question. Where'd you go to high school?

"Cathedral."

"When'd you graduate?" I ask.

"1960."

And I just about puke. The guy I thought was seventy-five at least, is only eight years older than I am. He's the same age as some of my friends.

My God. Eight years? Jesus, eight years ago Clinton was getting blowjobs in the White House. Eight years? Eight years is nothing. This old guy who sweats uncontrollably, this guy with the spillover belly and liver spots and a drinking man's nose, this guy killing time watching dogs run in circles is only eight years older than I am? Oh my God.

I need to be alone. I go upstairs to the balcony and I think about my father and my grandfather. I think about the old men watching TV screens and the old men working their secret systems, and the sweet old man who tried to explain what was so obvious on the big board. I think about the angry little man and the dogs never catching the colonel. I think about the young girls at the counter who didn't talk to old people. Who didn't talk to me. Who didn't even look at me.

I don't want to be old. I don't want to kill time. I want to be happy.

A guy who looks like a fat Kurt Vonnegut stumbles by, "Son of a bitch, goddamned dogs," he mutters.

A middle-aged woman with a fine Christian cross around her neck says to her husband as they walk down the stairs to the lower level, "These fucking dogs suck."

And that stupid damned bird from my first day here has found its way into the balcony and sits on the windowsill again.

I don't wait for him to figure out how to leave.

I walk down the stairs and out to my car. I don't want to come back.

I email Claudia out in Kanab.

God Bless America
and Breakfast Burritos to Go

Saturday August 20, 2005

I'm fifty-four years old, deep into a college teaching career that doesn't thrill me anymore, and heading to Utah to talk with someone who seems to have unlocked the mystery of how to change life in midstream. Right now I'm driving to Waco, Texas, and soon heading to Crawford, part-time home of our 43rd president. I hadn't thought about coming to Waco or Crawford until four hours into my trip, when I heard an overnight radio-jerk back in Pennsylvania call Cindy Sheehan, the woman at Bush's ranch protesting the Iraq War, the bitch in the ditch. I changed my route and headed south.

Waco is eighteen hundred miles from my home in Massachusetts. The first fifteen hundred miles were on interstate highways. (Here's how your get from my house to Texarkana—take a left at the end of my street, a right onto I-91, a right onto I-84, a left onto I-81, and a right onto I-40.) From inside my car one place has looked like another: New England looks like New York, which looks like Virginia, which looks like Tennessee. Target, Century 21, Costco, and Home Depot are sprinkled everywhere, and Walmart is a plague. North-to-south, food is homogenized: McDonalds (of course), Pizza Hut, Wendy's, Olive Garden, Ruby Tuesdays, TGI-Friday, and Cracker Barrel. Aside from the asshole who passed me a half hour east of Memphis at five in the morning and heaved a full can of Budweiser that exploded like a fat bug on my windshield, people have been uniformly friendly.

Waitresses are the friendliest of all. They smile, and talk to me, and make me feel at home. Hooray for waitresses!

But then there's the radio. Jesus. The drive through the South has been a constant buzz of angry, victim Christianity. We have those stations in Massachusetts too, but you have to search for them. Rush Limbaugh, a three-times divorced, drug addicted, ball of goo—the man who decides right and wrong for AM America— is the only non-Christian show I can pick up and when I listen to him, and not the other guys, it's almost like I'm listening to a reasonable, thoughtful voice. On station after station, an actor-grandfather instructs his actor-grandkids about God and Truth; which was followed by an ad pitching an anti Darwin book ("If you've ever wanted a simple and easy way to understand why evolution is wrong, this is for you!"); which was followed by another ad hawking a display that your kids can put on their school desks so they can piss off their (lying, scheming, Godless) science teachers. Truth and Glory as Product, sold with all the fervor and cleverness that Budweiser sells beer, or Pfizer sells Viagra.

Jimmy Swaggart, the sanctimonious evangelist who's been caught more than a couple times soliciting twenty-dollar prostitutes (followed by cloying apologies to his worldwide TV congregation), was on the radio as I drove past the exit for Bill Clinton's hometown of Hope, Arkansas. A half hour later I drove through Texarkana, the hometown of Clinton's special prosecutor and moral hector, Ken Starr. All of this reminds me just how close, all across the South, Big Religion and Big Sin are. One side can't exist without the other even though each side wants the other dead.

The last three hundred miles to Waco have been off the interstate and I agree with Least Heat Moon, life on the blue highways is better. Near Tyler, a business sign reads: "Dry Cleaners-Tire Store-Beer Tavern." Later, another business sign says: "Beer-Guns-Auto Upholstery." And another: "Be a Bunny, Buy a Gun for Your Honey." Then there's the sign for the Eagle Café: "American Owned and Proud." Underneath is a hand painted sign, "CLOSED."

In East Texas, the land from Big Sandy and Gilmer and all the way to Tyler is covered by an almost-Disney-designed-tiny-pine-forest. The world beneath the miniature trees is flat and the few streams and rivers I cross, especially the Sabine, seem to sit as puddles. Even though the place appears to be built for elves, real full-sized people live here and, from what they tell me, they seem to like it. So do I, and I don't know why. It isn't pretty, but I like it the way I like a low budget movie—nothing fancy, no great panoramic views, no over-the-top production values, just the essentials. And I have this idea that holds up even after I get back home and have a chance to think it through; with home, and relationships, and most important things, it's the quirks you need to love (the scrubby trees), not the good stuff (perfect lawns or paydays) because the quirks *are* home, *are* the person. The stuff that's the way you always hoped it would be is just gravy.

Finally, Waco. I'm tired and hungry, and sitting in La Fiesta Restaurant waiting for a waitress to take my order. It's Saturday night, and the place is wall-to-wall people. A lawyer-looking guy in dressy jeans and a red blazer is working the crowd. Couples my age, probably married forever, ignore each other as they eat enchiladas. A table of ten Mexican-American kids on a group date sit near me. They scan cellphones, laugh loud, drink large Pepsis, smile a lot, take many pictures of each other, are crisply dressed, say please and thank you and sir and ma'am, and except for their extreme politeness and skin they could be my kids.

My waitress is in her late teens, just about my son's age. She's blonde, slim, smiling, and sweating profusely. Her right wrist has a black brace on it. I ask what's wrong and she says, "Carpal Tunnel?" in that soft Southern manner that makes it sound as if she's asking a question. When she comes back with water I ask her if George Bush has ever eaten here, seeing as how his ranch is a half hour away.

"I'm not sure? But I'll check for you?"

"No, really, you don't have to, I was just curious," I say. She replies with gobs of courtesy,

"It's OK. Don't worry. I'll be right back?" And she's off on a mission, scurrying back to the kitchen where I can see her asking a couple of the older hands my question. She makes her way back to the dining area carrying a couple plates of food for another table—

her wrist must hurt like hell—and comes back with the answer. "No, he's never been here, but Jessica Simpson has? I waited on her seven times? She's from over in Killeen? And she's so nice? Oh, I just love her? But her uncle isn't so nice. I used to work at the Pizza Hut, and he'd come in and want free pizza? Can you believe that? And I'd tell him, 'You might be related to a famous person, but that doesn't mean that I have to give you free anything.'" I love waitresses.

I eat dinner, leave a good tip, and drive out to Crawford to see the Cindy Sheehan protest.

At eleven o'clock, about 16 miles past Waco, under the deep quiet of a dark prairie night—sharp stars, and the moon a shade less than full—I turn off the radio, roll down the window, now quiet both inside and out—and come to the crossroad that's the town of Crawford, Texas. In front of me on the northwest corner, on a platform that tops out at about ten feet, is a lighted display of two five-foot-tall plastic tablets of the Ten Commandments. Between them is a plastic Liberty Bell not quite as tall. A sign on the building behind it reads, "Camp Qualls," and I don't know if I'm in the right place. I thought the place was called "Camp Casey," after Cindy Sheehan's dead son, Casey.

I do a U-turn farther up Main Street, and slowly head back to the crossroad. A group of men about my age are on the southwest corner. They're dressed in black, sitting in dim light under a tarp, beside a circle of motorcycles. Eight pickup trucks are parked across the street. Hand-painted signs ring the small campsite;

most say "Freedom Isn't Free." And I'm confused. They don't look like anti-war, anti-Bush protestors.

Nearby, a few more trucks going nowhere circle the town. Then I see the POW MIA black flag and, of course, realize (it's funny how one little firm awareness can snap every formerly loose observation into place) that these people across the street from the religious symbols bracketing American symbols, are here to protest the protest.

I drive up and down the street again, watching them as they watch me. Something is going to happen. Maybe not here. Maybe not soon. But something is going to happen. Some clash, some conflict, some bang or pop. Somewhere. Sometime.

Sunday August 21, 2005

A "Future Farmers of America" sign welcomes me to Crawford. Year old red, white, and blue "Bush-Cheney '04" signs dot most front yards.

I shouldn't feel funny about having a small Honda with Massachusetts plates, but I do. I'm wishing I had a truck, a really big truck, screaming Alabama, or Georgia, or Tennessee. I also wish I had something other than a Red Sox hat for my bald head that's already sweating under a vicious sun, and it's only eight in the morning. Last night's men in black are here today under the same blue tarp, motorcycles parked nearby, POW MIA flags drooping.

Thinking Camp Casey must be somewhere around here, I park my car facing the shrine to Jesus and The War. A man from the black shirts marches toward me. I hop out of my car feeling like I just got pulled over by the State Police, fumble with my ink-stained backpack, trying not to make eye contact, hoping he'll keep walking. And of course, the man stops.

"Where you from?" he says in a flat tone.

"Back east."

"Where back east?"

"Massachusetts."

"Where 'bouts?"

"Not Boston."

"Where?"

"Springfield."

"No kidding, I'm from Windsor, Connecticut. Name's Bob."

"I'm Rick."

Turns out we grew up about ten miles apart, are roughly the same age, and both think that Big Al Anderson and the Wildweeds, a band from Bob's hometown, was the best Rock and Roll band no one ever heard of. Bob says he knows a guy from Springfield. The name sounds familiar, but I just can't remember.

"Yeah, that happens to me, too. Getting old, I guess." We shake hands.

Bob hates the guys on left. Thinks they're stupid, naïve at best, outright traitors at worst. He has his logic, "We spent 200 years fighting the bad guys to keep people free—little countries, big countries—never mattered." And he ticks off a list starting with England and France and ending with Afghanistan and Iraq, but forgetting Vietnam and Nicaragua and Chile and Iran and Grenada and others I'm forgetting.

"These guys in the ditch don't know what we're in for. What was 9/11, for God's sake? They're out to kill us. They attacked us and those idiots don't even know it." He's adamant, committed, rabid. He's more than mistrusting of the mainstream media, too. "You can't tell me only three thousand people got killed that day. You know how many people worked in those buildings? It's a cover up."

There's no arguing with Bob. So, I don't. I make oblique references to the protesters, say they might have a point, but he'll have none of it, and returns to the first thing he said, "They don't know what they're in for." He does, however, make one seriously strong argument about Cindy Sheehan's protest, "Her kid was killed but he was a grown man and he signed up twice."

Then Bob comes right out and asks me, "You for this war?"

I tell him the truth; that America should have gone to Afghanistan, if that's where he was, caught that fuck Bin Laden, cut off his nuts, slathered his nuts in pork fat and bacon, stuffed them in his mouth, staked him out on the sand, let him bake to death in the sun, and then get the hell out.

Bob seems to like that. "What about Iraq?"

Iraq is dumb. Wicked dumb. Sticking-your-hand-in-a-running-lawnmower dumb, and I would not fight there. I also do not want my eighteen-year-old son, my eighteen-year-old nephew, my twenty-one-year old daughter, or anyone else I know to fight there. I say that we have fought a bad war, that there are no weapons of mass destruction, that too few people speak the language, who know the culture, who are comfortable with their ways, but now that we're there, and have pretty much fucked the place up, it would be inhospitable to turn around and leave the party without asking the host if we could help tidy up.

"Yeah, I see what you mean. A lot of people think we didn't have enough troops," Bob says.

I'm on a roll. "If we were serious about this, and we're not, we'd have a draft and take about ten million young men and women, lots of rich kids, and Senators' sons and daughters—hell, take the Senators, too—and start at one border, and walk shoulder to shoulder to the other border, and wipe out the bad guys. Every one of them. But we're not serious. Hell, we don't even know who the bad guys are." Apparently, I have established my credentials and mean what I've said, except like I just said, I also think invading Iraq, which had nothing to do with 9/11 and had no big booming weapons, and posed no threat to us, was about as helpful to a so-called war on terror as invading Iceland.

Having been checked out, Bob takes me across the street to meet his comrades, all of whom are dressed in black, and look like Bob. Bob turns me around and introduces a man who doesn't look like they do. He's dressed in golfing colors; whites and powder blue, with cantaloupe-colored hair and pale skin turning a painful shiny red under the hot, unfiltered Texas sun. He sweats profusely. He tells me that he has recently finished writing a book and is trying to sell it. I'm glued. "Really, what about?" I ask, hoping for a writerly conversation.

"I was on the fifty-first floor of the North Tower." He hands me a card with his name on it and tells me his story.

"I was transferred from Bainbridge Island, Washington to New York City in early September, and was in my new job a week when the planes hit." He was thrown against a wall and it took more than an hour to climb down the stairs to escape. The experience shook him to his bones and rearranged everything in his world. How could it not?

"They attacked us," he says, using the same unidentified "they" that everyone dressed in black has used.

I have no words. I can't disagree with him, even though I do. I can't say that his experience is wrong, because it isn't. His experience is his experience. It's his conclusion, that we must attack Iraq, that's wrong. It's as if being close to, or actually in, the fire gives him a special perch from which to see when, in fact, his was likely the worst seat in the house.

I tell him about my neighbor, a twenty-two-year-old kid who was a flight attendant on the plane that hit just above him. God, it feels so wrong to speak of Jean, blasphemy really, to use her death to weasel out of an argument.

All of us (Bob, the black shirts, Cantaloupe man, and me) talk for close to half an hour, and take pictures of each other in front of the Ten-Commandments-Liberty-Bell-display. Oddly, Bob and I have bonded. He tells me his sister back home disagrees with him about the war and most other issues, "We don't talk about real stuff anymore." Kind of like me with Bob.

I say goodbye, get in my car and leave for the protest I came to see. Eight miles, and I'm here. Plastic crosses line the roadside to my left. They are small, no more than ten inches tall; begin in rows of one or two, and travel for fifty yards, widening closer toward the camp. Each cross carries a name, and there are many, many crosses.

One of the crosses on the road is for Cindy Sheehan's son, Casey. I learn that another cross, which has been removed three or four times and keeps being replanted by the protesters, is for Louis Qualls, the dead son of Gary Qualls, the man who put up the Christian-America exhibit at the crossroads in town. I also learn that a nearby rancher has driven his truck through the small forest of crosses, knocking down many, breaking some, and damaging all. Another man fires his shotgun into the night sky to scare the protesters.

The space that has looked so big on television is small, just a triangle in a dirt road. On one side a half dozen pro-war-pro-Bush people stand neat and orderly under the shade of another blue tarp. On the other side are forty or so anti-war-anti-Bush people housed in a tumble of tents, with composting areas, and recycling bins, and communal water. A hand-painted sign reads "Camp Casey."

A yellow crime-scene tape separates the groups so that the space in mid-triangle is a demilitarized zone of sorts. Each side ignores the other, but once in a while someone will nod a small hello. A state trooper meanders between the two groups, keeping the peace and moving the small flow of traffic around, which seems like an easy enough job.

Numbers are down today. Possibly because it is Sunday, a day of rest for everyone. More likely it's because the main attraction, Cindy Sheehan, is in California tending to her mother who just had a stroke. I walk around the triangle taking pictures, and kneel to read more names on the crosses. It's a strange, disconnected weirdness to read a hand-scribbled name on a little plastic cross and realize it's a person who has left circles of people in tears, and possibly children who will someday ask, "Who's that?"

About an hour later, I go for a run down to the closed-off road that leads to Bush's ranch. I haven't eaten in anticipation of the run and stupidly haven't had more than a mouthful or two of water either. There isn't a thermometer out here but it's at least a hundred degrees.

I run along the side of the road, smiling and laughing to myself, and recording every random thought I have on the mini-tape recorder I hold in my left hand. Cars drive by and every single one waves to me, and it doesn't matter whether they have a "Bush for President" bumper sticker, an "Out of Iraq" sign, or it's the county sheriff. I'm reminded that waving to strangers is one of the things I like about the south and west, and one of the things I do not like at all about the north and east.

I'm feeling the heat and slowing down. My face is hurting. I've been working on a sinus headache for two days and on this run it seems to come to fruition, sliding from the top of my skull to the back of my eyes, to my cheek bones, to my jaw, and into my teeth. The small irritation in my chest that I've been feeling for the past month makes an appearance and I, of course, think I'm about to have a heart attack. What a stupid goddamned trick of nature it would be to die near George Bush's ranch, at the Cindy Sheehan protest, when she's not even here.

Two Texas State Troopers in a patrol car guard the barricade to the Bush ranch. The passenger-side trooper gets out and stands tall and wide in Nike sneakers, jeans, and a tan golf shirt. He is easily six-feet-four and probably weighs two-forty, two-fifty, and if there is fat on him it is very well hidden. I must look like shit because he asks if I'm okay, and if I need a ride someplace.

"I'm fine, just not used to the heat." Then I ask him what he thinks about the demonstration back up the road, and if there's been any trouble.

"It's one country. It's their right," he says.

Back at Camp Casey. Because I've stopped sweating my shirt and shorts quickly begin to dry. I'm dehydrated and feel wobbly. A woman offers me water from the communal ice chest, "You ran down to the barricade? In this? Take a couple waters. You sure you're OK?" I tell her I'm fine, but I'm not.

I feel better, but not good, and begin walking around the triangle again. I meet a woman from Cape Cod who's about ten years younger than I am. My Red Sox cap is a magnet. She's out here for the same reason everyone else (but me) is, to protest. She's envious of us who are older, and have antiwar stories to tell about the old days. She asks, so I tell her mine—arrest-court-jail-X2— then pose for a picture with her, and walk on.

A young guy, probably mid-twenties, just back from Iraq and his stint as a guard at the torture site, Abu Ghraib Prison, is at the protest hoping to be cleansed. He is fragile, nearly broken. He says he wants to change back to who he used to be. I wish him luck, but think what he hopes for is about the hardest thing there is to do, to go back to the way things were. We shake hands. He doesn't want to let go.

A woman from Washington State and I are vying for the longest drive. I think she wins, but not by much. I tell her I met a man in Crawford who's from Bainbridge Island, and her face widens into a smile, "Great, maybe he'd want to drive back with us."

I say, "He's on the other side of the street under the blue tarp." I point to him, call out his name, and wave. "Right there, the guy with the orange hair," I say, and her smile droops to a sour frown. I explain to her that he was on the fifty-first floor of the North Tower when the first plane hit, and she says, "Well then, he should know what the truth is," as if there is one truth, as if that one truth can be known. Next to my cantaloupe friend, a tall, thin man wrapped head to toe in flowing gauze, silently holds two signs that say 9/11 happened because we haven't outlawed abortions.

I go back to the ice chest, open another water, and start a conversation with three people around my age. Connie (the only name I remember) is originally from the Upper Peninsula Michigan, and now lives in Texas, over in Palestine. The man is also from Michigan, and the other woman is from Florida. Connie asks me if I'm retired. I must look awful.

The four of us hit it off. We talk about the old times; the 60's, and the protest marches, and the music, and how this feels so much like those days, but really very different, too. I joke that the biggest difference is we're all older than our parents were back then, and we look like hell with our lumpy bodies, varicose veins, shiny scalps, and hairy ears. They ask me if college kids are protesting the war, and I tell them that the students are bored by it all, and act as if this were happening to a different country, not their own. Without a draft they feel no danger, and consequently have little personal stake in the outcome.

Connie says they're headed for the second Camp Casey, which is a total surprise to me because I've only heard about this one.

"Yeah, there's another site a few miles from here. The man who fires his shotgun every night has a cousin nearby who's a Vietnam vet. He donated part of his land to the cause." Now that's courage.

Instead of having them wait for the Camp Casey Shuttle, I suggest they jump in my car. We drive through pastures, and ranch land, and past the State Troopers who offered to help me. "Good guys," I say, and we all wave.

"Oh, did I tell you? Joan Baez is playing tonight," Connie says, making it the 60's all over again.

The second Camp Casey is a huge complex, the center of which is an eight-post tent that looks exactly like the Denver Airport. It is massively Tee-Pee-ish and appears out of nowhere. Outside the tent are many, many portable toilets and many, many wash tables with pump bottles of sanitizing gel to clean hands before protesting.

The grounds are neat, tidy, and of course sanitary; a place for everything and everything in its place, as if OSHA or the PTA had put this together. A half dozen tents outside the main tent are reserved for TV, radio, and newspapers reporters where they can interview subjects out of this crazy-hot sun. There's a small field of plastic crosses, just like back at the first camp, only this one has perfect geometrical spacing, which makes it look like a Lilliputian Arlington National Cemetery. Two television people and a cameraman walk right through the shrine on their way to the interview tents.

The big tent feels larger inside than it looks from outside. I pace it off at fifty yards long and thirty-five yards wide, half a football field. Walls are lined with posters, and signs from various groups against the war: Iraqi Vets, Vietnam Vets, mothers, socialists, and a group of Christians who, from what I can tell, might be the last handful of Christians in America who have read the kinder, gentler New Testament. Two priests give a Sunday Service and offer communion. Four Black people, the only Black people I've seen today, all in their sixties, sit by themselves in a small circle. Closer to the stage are candles and flowers. Huge round tables that comfortably seat a dozen people are set up, banquet style, in the rear quarter of the tent.

Connie waves me over. "Free Lunch," she says, and I follow her to the buffet line where there are the usual luncheon buffet items: chips, and lunch meat, slices of cheese, and bowls of tuna salad, and chicken salad, and pita, and water rolls, and good crusty bread. There's also a giant salad of mixed micro-greens with just-picked-this-morning-tomatoes ringing the bowl. We have our choice of four different Paul Newman salad dressings. There's an interesting dish of potato, onion, and mushroom, sautéed with rosemary and garlic (I go back for seconds); there's also a ragout of locally grown vegetables (more seconds); and something called King Ranch lasagna which looks like regular lasagna except made with tortillas instead of pasta (I pass). There are red olives, and green olives, and Kalamata olives in olive oil, and more cheeses—the feta is wonderful—and pecans, and walnuts, and almonds, and there is organic peanut butter, and hot tea, and iced tea, and coffee, and energy drinks, and fresh spring water, and lemons for the fresh spring water. A refrigerated truck is outside next to a smaller tent that serves as a kitchen to keep the bowls filled and the people happy. Olive oil drips from my lips. I am stuffed.

There's no salt. There are no waitresses. I miss both.

I can feel the day beginning to slip away. It's afternoon, and I have miles to go before I sleep, I hope in New Mexico, over in Roswell if I can make it by midnight. Connie assures me that they'll be OK with the shuttle. We all say goodbye, and I drive out of the compound heading toward New Mexico, now only half of Texas away.

The world past Crawford looks much more western; it's wide and broad with deep vistas of scrubbiness whenever the road rises, which is becoming less and less frequent. The blue sky has gotten even bigger, and it is road-shimmering hot. About eighty miles beyond Crawford, on Route 36, just outside of Comanche, there's a sign for the "Deep Shit Cattle Company." I laugh, which brings up a strong feta and olive burp. I shake my head at my luncheon experience. Protest politics as a catered event? Tastefully garnished with sprigs of rosemary and bunches of mint? What happened to Sproul Plaza? Selma? Chicago? Orangeburg? Kent State? What happened to Woodstock?

The drive is becoming repetitive. I'm reminded of kid cartoons where the background scene is a loop showing the same three-second sequence over and over again, while Fred or Barney or the Roadrunner moves his feet in a blur. Here, on Route 180, west of Anson, just past Abilene, there is nothing-nobody-nothing-nobody, just miles and miles of nothing and nobody; the circular scene altered only by a dead snake on the side of the road, thump-thump-dead. The road rises, just the least little bit, and the loop breaks in the distance where scattered munchkin trees, seemingly dropped without order, stand among fields of yellow wildflowers.

There's an awful lot of Texas, so damned much earth in every direction. Back home there are trees that block short views, and hills that block long views, and houses surround houses, and people seem to feel unimportant, I think, largely because there are so many of us in such small parceled spaces. Land must shape perception. Back east, we tend to be short with people; quick and hurried, pushy, as if we are always trying to break free of some sort of confinement. People out here don't seem to be like that; they wave me through at intersections, they hold doors, they say hello, and call me *sir*. Life is slower, smaller inside the bigness of the land. Maybe we're different because the worlds are different.

Who knows? But it gets me thinking about George Bush and how he had to occupy these two worlds as a kid; tony New England prep school, then Yale and Harvard, and summers in Maine at the family compound on the ocean; and then home here in Midland Texas, in the Permian Basin, where oil is king, hands are calloused, and showers are taken after work, not before. Suddenly the uncomfortable look he gives off—the squirminess, the forced cackle, practiced shoulder shrugs—make some sense to me. Maybe he doesn't fit. Maybe he knows it. Maybe he's always trying to be one of the guys because he isn't. Maybe his words are clumsy because instead of just being George, he has to think about where he is, who he's with, and how he's supposed to act. Maybe he wasn't comfortable in either place without some rehearsed role to grease the skids—drunk guy, wise guy, good old boy, brush-clearing cowpoke standing tall, arms wide like a gunslinger. He is so wrongly Darwinian, survival by *trying* to fit, instead of just being George.

If the guy were truly confident and had instincts he could trust, he'd get on his mountain bike and unannounced, ride down to the big tent, stand on the stage all sweaty, and cool-looking, and say what the state trooper said to me: that he's glad people are here, glad we're all Americans, hope they enjoy Crawford, and then he'd get in the buffet line, pick a crowded table and chow down. "Mmmm … damned good feta. Now where's those Kalamata olives I been hearing so much about?" And the demonstration would be over just like that. But he can't do it. And the war on terror goes on.

Sunday August 21, 2005

Sixty miles south of Lubbock, off to my right, is a butte, perfectly formed but in miniature. I'll drive hours before I see another and the next one will be much bigger. This one stands orphaned, alone for many miles, as if it wandered away from its family in a slow motion, glacial time crawl until it sat down, beaten, completely lost, and unable to get home.

In Post, Texas I pull into a McDonalds to pee, music from the Rocky Horror Picture Show is playing. On the way out I stop at the counter to buy a Coke.

"What size?" the counter kid asks.

"Medium, I guess."

"That'll be a dollar fifty-nine. But you can super-size it for seventy-five cents."

I give the kid two thirty-four.

"No sir. You pay seventy-five cents." And he hands me back a dollar fifty-nine. Which is how I came to be drinking a forty-two-ounce Coca Cola which lasts across the rest of west Texas, through places like Tokio, Tahoka, Brownfield, and Bronco, and past every crossroad that looks like the final scene from *Castaway* where Tom Hanks has to choose his future. I zoom past dead little movie theaters in dead little towns, and this is another movie, *The Last Picture Show*; a wasteland of empty storefronts and busted businesses. Steinbeck's dust is everywhere. Bugs are hitting my windshield like a protein storm. Giant towers run along the highway, and they look like one angular massive cowboy after another; standing high-shouldered, arms wide, electric wire as rope stringing them all together. No, wait … they look like George Bush tries to look.

Hooray New Mexico! A longhorn steer stands off to my right just across the state line and sunset is dead ahead. Cars come infrequently from the opposite direction. In twilight, I count when I first see a headlight: one Mississippi, two Mississippi … three hundred Mississippi. I can see cars at least ten miles away. With this wide, flat land I feel like I'm riding on the earth, really riding *on* the earth. For the first time in my life, I'm aware that I'm an earthling.

There's a haze of light to the west, not actual light, just light residue. I'm twenty-five miles away but it's probably Roswell, UFO capital of the world. And to make the scene even better than the Chamber of Commerce could have ordered, on the radio is the George Noory syndicated talk show having a serious academic discussion of flying saucers. It makes me look up into the sky, but the only peculiar thing I see are flames near the northern horizon, which turn out to be gas burning off oil wells. This is perfect.

I cross the Pecos River and in a few minutes, enter Roswell population 45,000; just a regular town with a wide Main Street, a sturdy courthouse, and signs everywhere saying, "Aliens Welcome." My grandfather would have loved this. Everyone in the family laughed at him when he said he once saw a UFO. They laughed even more when he said he saw hippos in the Chesapeake Bay. He'd feel right at home here. He drank some.

Monday Morning August 22, 2005

I'm not sure what I expected the UFO Museum to look like: Perhaps a disk-shaped building in the desert. Maybe something misty with fog machines and lights blinking to musical tones like the movie, *Close Encounters of the Third Kind*. At least a geodesic dome. But for the moment the UFO Museum (Research Center and Hall of Fame) is housed in an old movie theater near the corner of Second and Main in downtown Roswell.

Inside, the place is a fifth-grade science project: Papier mache spaceships, rocks that look like ET, drawings of rockets, and affidavits swearing to God all this is true. A large man and I wander through the museum, in step and silent. Finally I ask where he's from. "West Virginia. Taking the RV over to Vegas in a day or two."

"Casinos?" I ask.

"No sir, Area Fifty-One." I'm perplexed, and he sees it. "That's where they took the space-vehicle after it crashed," he says with complete conviction.

"Right, Area Fifty-One," I say.

"Been out there a couple times. Great place to eat right nearby. You like chicken-fried steak?"

We both pause to pay our respects at the glassed-in, life-sized display of the dying, or dead (I can't be certain which) alien lying on a hospital gurney. It's being examined by a doctor in a white coat, and looming over them is a more ominous figure (military intelligence?) in a black suit, black hat and white surgical mask. A terrible burn between the legs of the wispy nude figure, who really does look remarkably like ET, seems to have burned off his or her genitals. The alien's nipples are untouched. I wonder why it has nipples. I wonder why I have nipples.

I stop in the gift shop on the way out, buy some junk, and talk with the cashier, a good green kid who's joining the National Guard next week. "How come?" I ask.

"So I can get my GED and get a good job when I get out." The boy's friend, who also joined the National Guard, just got sent to Iraq, but the recruiter said it won't happen to this boy because he's going to be an MP.

I lean across the counter, shake the boy's hand, and wish him luck. "Be safe," I say.

"Oh, don't worry about me, sir. The man told me I won't go, and I believe him."

Near the lobby, about fifteen feet from the boy who believes he won't go to Iraq, are five reasons why the government has covered up alien visits. Reason number four is that religions and true believers would go nuts if there was evidence that we were not alone in the universe.

I leave the museum and get a cup of tea across the street at the Not of This World Christian coffee shop. The woman who owns the place looks only at her computer screen where she plays a never-ending game of solitaire. Next door, at a gift shop, I buy a plaque—"Roswell, The Truth Lives Here." An hour later, driving north out of town on Main Street, I see the courthouse again, this time in daylight. The Ten Commandments are etched on two large stone tablets.

I suppose it's good to believe, no matter what you believe. And Roswell has managed to believe nearly everything.

Monday Afternoon August 22, 2005

The cold white clouds and the sharp blue sky, make it feel as if I'm under Arctic water, looking up at icebergs. Small ranches with makeshift ponds and leaning-to-one-side outbuildings pop up every few miles, and sheep and cattle graze in clusters.

There are few things in life better than this—listening to Neil Young on the CD player, driving into the dark pink of New Mexico, moving through beautiful scrub that changes to grassland, and thinking back to traveling with my college drop-out friends, Chip and Tony, seeing the Southwest for the first time. How nuts we were, joyously screaming and yelling, stopping the car by the side of the road, and tumbling down an embankment to play Frisbee in the first dried up riverbed we saw. If I had a Frisbee I'd stop the car and do it again.

I have my first sight of mountains near the town of Vaughn, elevation 5900 feet. A town is small when it puts the elevation on its sign instead of its population. Vaughn looks only a little better than hard-broken Bronco back in Texas. There's a sign in a diner window, "Female Vocalist Wanted," and I start thinking about how important it is to honor dreams. My son, for instance, wanting to be a musician. How simple it would be to kill his hope. "Where are you going to get a job? What can you do with a degree in music?"

What the hell? Go for it. I wish I had. But now in my middle fifties, something seems to be stirring in me, like I was eighteen again and looking out at life wide-open. If I could sing (and was a woman) I think I'd answer the ad.

Encino has a post office on Main Street, but everything else looks closed—hardware store, dry goods store, a motel under "New Menagment" (spelled exactly that way), and out of business for at least fifteen years.

A miles-long train chugs by. Elk signs appear, they look like muscular deer, and this sign, along with a million other signs just like it, has been the victim of a drive-by shooting. Mexican hip-hop is on the radio until I hit *seek*, and find, voila! Taj Mahal from back home in Springfield, singing a Bluesy-Caribbean song that makes me smile so much my face hurts.

I want to stay in Santa Fe if I can find the damned place. There are signs for it, but the exits fly by, and I don't know which to take, so I just pick one, and in a mile or two I am on a highway with no way off, so I keep driving. A billboard says the singer, Don Ho, is performing at the Camera Rock Casino next week. For a few months in 1950, he was a Phys Ed student at the college in Massachusetts where I teach. He went back home to Hawaii when the first snow hit. If he'd stayed, he might have been a gym teacher singing the hell out of songs in the echo chamber of a high school shower. Later, a flashing sign at the Casino says, The Don Ho Show is Cancelled Until Further Notice. I zoom through a town whose name I can't pronounce until I get home and look it up; Pojoaque (pe-wa-ki), proud home of the Elks and the Elkettes.

Los Alamos is the next town, about ten miles ahead, straight up a winding road of cutbacks. On my left, cars curve down the mountain, and to my right, on the other side of the guardrail, the road falls straight-away, a thousand feet below. Rain is falling, soft in stretches, only hard every now and then. My eyes skip across the valley to the ridiculous beauty of pink rocks and changing shadows spreading under the darkening clouds. I drift into downhill traffic, then swerve back to my lane. My stomach drops. My palms sweat all the way to Los Alamos, half a mile higher than the highest place back home in New England. Thunder rolls across the mountains like distant bombs, and the coincidence of that sound in this town, where the first Atomic Bombs were made, unsettles me.

I drive around Los Alamos, home of the Manhattan Project— passing streets like Trinity, Oppenheimer, and Bikini—and pull into the parking lot behind the Bradbury Science Museum. The place is clean and modern, with angled walls painted every shade of red I've seen in New Mexico. I buy a ticket, walk in, and before I know it I'm crying, almost sobbing, and I cannot believe how quickly this feeling rises, how strong it is, how I don't really care who sees me. The two reasons for these tears, this museum, this town, and perhaps the state of the world, sit almost next to each other—Fat Man and Little Boy. They are usual, unimpressive, mundane; like you could fill them with propane, hook them to a couple of grills and barbecue pork chops for your neighbors. And these things started it all? This is what we're afraid of? They have caulking like my bathtub has caulking. They have nuts and bolts and metal and screws the way all dumb things have nuts and bolts and metal and screws.

I stop near Fat Man to watch a 3x5 video of men loading the original white metal bulb onto a plane. There's a bulls-eye painted on the nose of the bomb with a message, "To Hirohito With Love and Kisses."

I cannot believe I'm watching this. I say to the small screen, "Don't do it. Stop," as if my voice could travel backward sixty years and sixteen days, and be so loud and so convincing that they would put the damned thing down and just walk away. But, I'm only an idiot in a museum talking to a three-minute loop of silent video playing on a screen the size of a notecard.

Just beyond the bombs is a timeline of the war, and I think of my father, the age of my son right now, fighting in the South Pacific, and how without the damned bombs he quite likely would have been one of many to die in the invasion of Japan. And I cry all over again because I cannot imagine him killing people, although he did; and I cannot imagine him dying, although he will in three years. Around the corner another panel shows that Eniwetok (Ānewetak), where my father fought, and probably killed people, became a nuclear testing site.

Near the exit are wall-sized pictures of Hiroshima and Nagasaki, and they are awful. Awful. Burned bodies, real bodies, not funny waif-like mannequins from this morning's diorama of the dead or dying alien in Roswell at the UFO Museum. These bodies are stiff and bloated, smoke rises off many, and other bodies certainly have been vaporized into the air. Poof. Gone. And some asshole is on his cellphone walking behind me talking business, loud—Get a quote on the price—and I want to turn around and punch him.

Three seats to my left, in the small movie theater where an eighteen-minute movie of the development of the Manhattan Project is showing, are a Japanese woman and a Japanese man who appear to be in their mid-sixties. They sit without tears or talk, without smiles or signs of sadness; their eyes straight ahead, unblinking at the screen as the pictures of mushroom clouds rise over Hiroshima and Nagasaki.

There is a pond in the middle of town in what was the middle of the Manhattan Project. It is called Ashley Pond, named after the man, Ashley Pond, Junior, who founded the Los Alamos Boys Ranch School that was once on this site. (The joke around town is that the pond really ought to be named Ashley Pond, Ashley Pond, Pond.) Because Ashley Junior had been sickly as a kid, and because rugged outdoor activity made him healthy (he grew to become one of Teddy Roosevelt's Roughriders), he wanted his school to have "nature as its textbook," so, he had his students dress in shorts year-round, sleep outside on screened-in porches no matter the weather, and swim YMCA style—naked—in the pond until it froze over, whereupon they would play hockey in tiny shorts and skates. The school produced a curious array of graduates. I cannot find the connecting thread, except for this long-gone school, that runs through Bill Veeck, William Burroughs, and Gore Vidal. Then the government closed it, tore down some buildings, let others stand, put up a town of Quonset huts, muddy roads, and scientists, and set about the business of building those two amazing goddamned bombs.

I walk slowly past the pond and the remaining buildings once used by the School and the Project. I stop every few minutes, overwhelmed, that on this spot everything, forever on earth, changed. I have never been to a place of such importance, never felt what I feel right here.

Across a parking lot, a boy about six or seven-years-old holds his mother's hand as they leave Fuller Lodge, the large log building that became the central meeting hall for the Manhattan Project, now the town community center. He wears a karate suit with a bright orange belt, exactly the color of his mother's hair. She fiddles with her cellphone as they walk to her minivan and drive away. Life, good mundane life, goes on as if nothing special happened here because, I suppose, what else is there?

Leaving town on switchbacks up a mountain into miles
of forest—five years ago blackened by an out-of-control,
government-controlled burn—fuzzy green life peeks up under
charcoal. Elk crossing signs are followed by (cue the elk) a herd
of elk crossing the road, and on this far side of the mountain, the
side with no fire, a road sign with a stick-figure reads, "Congested
Area," but other than fifteen cars an hour ago on the fringe of Los
Alamos, I've seen no cars and no people.

This is the most beautiful place on earth I've never heard of.
Valles Caldera is a miles-wide bowl a million years old, cuddled
under hills; and down below, where the volcano blew, animals
graze on thick grass and bellow their sounds away before the
sounds bounce back. It's not a striking and severe beauty of rocks
and angles like the rest of New Mexico; just a large, lush, every
shade of green, never want to leave it, beauty.

I feel no world outside of this valley: no job, no Crawford, no
Iraq, no UFOs, no Little Boy, no Fat Man, no Fat Rush, no yelling,
no preaching, no headache, no thoughts, no jokes, no nothing.
Maybe not even me. It's just back of the moon quiet, broken by
the occasional elk snort.

A few miles later, at the next pedestrian crossing where no
pedestrians cross, someone has stuck an ET face on the head of
the crossing pedestrian, and it's funny. Farther down the road,

someone has shot a deer crossing sign, which, after many shot deer signs, is not funny.

I ask directions from the man who owns a general store at the Y in the road. One way is seventy miles and paved, the other is forty and not.

"Which way should I go?"

"Either way," he says.

"How long will it take?" I ask.

The man shrugs, "Dirt's more interesting." He is Zen.

The dirt road goes washboard just as a garbage truck rumbles by kicking up dust, and pebbles, and stink. An old lady walks alongside the road pushing on a cane. She smiles and we wave. A kid truck driver drives gingerly. We also wave. At five miles per hour, curving back and forth on switchbacks, through forests, past small streams, and ponds, and piles of elk droppings, I eventually rise 10,000 feet. A giant tree, two feet from the road has burnt, root to branch. Trees surrounding it are bright green. I don't know why, but this one is the prettiest of all. I stop my car in the middle of the road, walk over and touch it.

On the other side of the mountain the dirt road is paved but under repair. A flag-woman at a road construction site tells me,

"The project should've been long done. But Walmart has first dibs on concrete."

I cross the continental divide where every drop of water falling left runs to the Pacific and every drop of water falling right runs to the Atlantic. Only left or right, no middle ground, no place to settle and collect. The land is dry and worn. One way or the other, just like America.

A Navajo radio station is on and I cannot understand a thing. Then I hear the DJ tell a joke in this language that's not mine, but I get the rhythm, and the timing—the set-up has a familiar feel, the punchline does, too. And then the laugh. And that's the same everywhere, isn't it? Why did the snake slither across the road? Thump-thump, dead now, never know.

Then it's Bloomfield, New Mexico and water in a river which is rare, and another Baptist Church which is not. Down the road are liquor stores, pawn shops, a racetrack and casino, and "The Adult Couples Mega Store." A "Jesus Is Watching You" billboard rises above it all. Behind that is a smaller billboard for "Do-It-Yourself Divorces, $250." We fish where there's fish.

Local radio news in English: "The school board decided last night that alternatives to evolution must be taught in all county schools." Lakota, Hopi, Navajo? Buddhist and Hindu? Muslim? Probably not. Probably just Baptist.

National radio news: "President Bush is in Idaho on vacation from his Crawford vacation, and evangelical TV preacher Pat Robertson said we should assassinate the President of Venezuela."

Sign in a diner window: "God Bless America and Breakfast Burritos to Go."

Tonight in Page, Arizona, I stay in a motel overlooking another concrete-eating Walmart. The earth is parched, the air is dry, but in the distance a few clouds and a perfect rainbow float over a completely out of place florescent green golf course. Tomorrow, in Kanab, Utah, I'll talk with Claudia, who changed her life in midlife. I want her to give me the answer.

"Don't force it. Just do what you like," she will say. For the past five days, I have.

Nick Takes the Wheel

Why am I driving to Carrizozo New Mexico, population 996? Because I like the name. Go ahead, say it with me. Care-a-ZO-ZO. Has a rhythm to it, doesn't it? Kind of like a nine-letter song? You can't say Carrizozo and be anything but happy. Anyway, that's the way it struck me over the winter when I was looking for a location for a story I'm trying to write about an out-of-place boy who was born near Roswell, New Mexico in 1947, the year the aliens crashed. I'm not exactly sure why the kid felt like he didn't belong; maybe because he looked odd, or that his family was strange, or that he and his father were so conflicted, but the only thing that made the kid feel good was thinking that he was from someplace else, like maybe Mars.

The plan is to spend a week in Carrizozo, pick up my nineteen-year-old son who's flying into Las Vegas and then make the cross-country trip with him that I'd always dreamt of doing but couldn't because life intervenes: work, divorce, shared custody, money, or lack of it.

I'm smiling and singing. Care-a-ZO-ZO.

My car is parked in Roswell, one block north of the UFO Museum (Hall of Fame, and Research Center). I love this place—the alien-face streetlights, the McDonalds UFO playscape, the completely ridiculous juxtaposition of The UFO Museum sitting directly across the street from a Christian coffee shop whose owner might have a hard time embracing the notion that we are all created in God's image—earthlings and aliens alike. I even love that this town, that only seems to be known to the larger world for the maybe-crash of an alien spacecraft, has a city hall that has the Ten Commandments on five-foot tall stone tablets in its front yard. The whole place reeks of joyous contradiction. I can't wait to show my son, Nick.

My phone rings. It's my ex-wife, Joanne. "Don't worry. Nick's in the hospital but he's going to be fine." I go cold. My muscles freeze. "Why? What happened? You sure he's okay?"

And he is okay, more or less. He was attacked and beaten, has a very swollen face, is bruised, and well-shaken. It seems one of Nick's friends met a girl online and she invited that kid, Nick and another kid to a party in her town, Greenwich, Connecticut, a couple hours south of where we live in Massachusetts. The local boys at the party didn't like the interlopers, and when Nick and his friends were leaving, they were jumped.

Joanne and I were married for not quite five years, and we've been divorced for eighteen. We ended things when Nick was barely a year-old. We have a daughter Chelsea, three years older than Nick, and Joanne has a daughter from her first marriage Jen, who was ten when we went to court. Joanne and I are two very different people who never should have married—she'd rather go to Epcot, I'd rather go to Italy. I don't want this story to be about us.

"You sure that's all?" I ask her.

"And he and his friends were arrested."

I hang up, get in my car, drive up and over some mountain, past some scenery, through some town where Billy the Kid escaped from jail, through some other town where Smoky Bear was found and raised, and then finally down the long road into the wide valley where Carrizozo sits. I barely notice things that would normally make me stop, poke around and yell *yippee*! I keep thinking about my son. I'm five days from home, feeling a helplessness that grabs my brain and twists it out of my head. I shout and punch the passenger seat. Goddammit. My eyes tear.

But this valley is beautiful. And from what I can see, Carrizozo is not. There's a grimy, splintered, ready-to-come-apart feel to it; broken fences, trash, boarded up buildings, and lots and lots of empty nips, like my grandfather used to carry around with him. I want to go home.

I call Joanne again. "Nick's gonna be okay, right? Should I come back?" He's at her house sleeping, has a headache, his face hurts, and the doctor said he'll need a week or ten days to get back to normal.

"Maybe you should push his flight back a week." Now I have two weeks in this dump of a town.

There are three motels in Carrizozo, all pretty much the same, and all at the intersection of highways 380 and 54, where Carrizozo's only stoplight sits. I pick the first motel I see because what difference does it make? The clerk at the desk, the wife of the husband-wife ownership team, asks where I'm from, and I say, "Springfield, Massachusetts," and she says, "Oh my God! I went to high school at MacDuffie's," a private school for girls on Maple Street in Springfield. "Small world," I say, not really wanting to talk. The room is clean enough, the bed is marginally sleepable, and my cell phone only works when I sit on the left corner of the bed near the door.

Back up highway 380 about a mile from the stoplight, there was a farm stand that sold local fruits and vegetables. I'm hungry and not eager to test the restaurant scene in Carrizozo (if there is a restaurant scene) so I drive back to the farm stand to get something to hold me over until supper. The cherries are wicked good, so are the local melons and plums. Because she sees my Massachusetts license plate, the woman running the stand tells me she's from Maine.

"Almost neighbors," she says.

Her name is Sheila. She's very talkative, very friendly and before I know it she tells me she is fifty, that she's been married three times, that she's been with her third husband for twenty-two years now, that she writes and sings and does voice-over work for radio stations because "Out here everyone here needs a few different jobs to get by." Sheila asks if I want to help move some furniture twelve miles north to an old schoolhouse in White Oaks where they're having a charity auction later in the week. "Come back in an hour."

I've only had one real rule that I follow on these around-the-country trips; unless I think I'm going to get killed, the default answer to all questions is, "Sure, what the hell." So, an hour later I'm back at the farm stand, packing Sheila's truck, and following her up highway 54, and then up a long winding road that, kind of, ends in a once-upon-a-time gold mining town, now virtual ghost town, of White Oaks.

A cowboy named Dan is supposed to meet us but he's late so we wait in a bar, a small place called The No Scum Allowed Saloon. An almost life sized painting of the five foot three-inch-tall Billy the Kid is on one wall, with dozens of old license plates are on another. On the ceiling are hundreds of dollar bills with scribbled messages on them. I squint but can't make out anything. Behind the bar, the tip jar is a human-sized mannequin wearing a tank top over large breasts and protruding nipples. Nick is going to love this place.

Sheila begins to tell me about her best friend, Ivy. "Amazing woman. Lives up the dirt road, built the house herself. Every man in Lincoln County's had a thing for her. Hell of a potter and you know what? The girl can roll a cigarette with one hand and throw back a shot of Jack Daniels with the other." And on cue, Ivy walks in, says hi to Sheila, nods in my direction, orders a shot of Jack, and begins rolling a cigarette.

Sheila nudges me, "Was I lying?"

I can't decide if Ivy is ugly or pretty. When I look at her one way I see a stunning woman in her late thirties—blonde hair, blue eyes, fair skin, small frame, and a spark of life that shimmers. I look again and think she's nearing seventy; lined and wrinkled and missing teeth, and maybe the blonde hair is really grey? I decide that Ivy is funny, smart and beautiful. She asks me why in hell someone would bother to come out this way. "White Oaks is a ghost town and Carrizozo ain't much better."

"Because I saw Carrizozo on a map and I liked the sound of it," I say.

She coughs a laugh of smoke. "So, where you from?"

"Springfield, Mass."

"Jesus, my first husband came from Chicopee. (The city just north of Springfield.) We came out here to ski. I stayed, he left. Know any people named Vogel?"

Cowboy Dan ambles in. He looks the way cowboy movie stars want to look; neatly pressed white cotton shirt buttoned to the neck and cuff, leather face and hands, old worn cowboy boots, weathered hat, jeans that could stand up by themselves, a seriously funny sense of humor, and a wicked smile under the bushy, droopy mustache. He rolls right into his spot-on impression of John Wayne as Boy George. "Do you really want to hurt me? Well, do ya pilgrim?" I'm on the floor laughing.

After Sheila, Dan, and I unload Sheila's truck, we head back to the No Scum and Ivy asks if Sheila and I want to come up to her place for a tour and supper. I give her my default answer, and after a four-mile drive up a dirt road that my little Honda wishes were paved, we come to Ivy's adobe house and pottery studio. "She built it herself," Sheila says again.

"Yup," says Ivy. "Had no idea how to make adobe but I apprenticed with an old guy for a couple years." The studio is beautiful, open and wide with two floors, one for her work and one for display. Her pieces are delicate and light, like they would fit perfectly in a New York gallery. Her house is tight and small, along the lines of a cabin on a boat. We cook and eat and laugh, talk a lot about getting older, and how our bodies are falling apart, teeth especially.

Ivy says, "My father said I ought to have the rest of my teeth pulled. But I told him I ain't gonna be the blowjob queen of Lincoln County and that settled that."

As I walk in the dark to my car, parked about thirty or forty yards away, Ivy says to watch out for bears. I laugh. "Not kidding," she says.

I talk to Nick the next day. He's okay but quiet. I can't get a read on him. Tired? Embarrassed? Sore? Just doesn't want to talk to me? I make a reservation—United flight 7667, 11:58 PM, Monday July 10, 2006, McCarran International Airport, Las Vegas.

A man is stooped over, pulling weeds from the small garden in front the local Chamber of Commerce, an out-of-place caboose situated on Central Avenue, Route 54. I make an inane comment, "Looking pretty," because my other rule for these trips around the country is to talk to everyone. Ray and his wife moved to Carrizozo a few years ago. He's a retired pharmacist from Ohio and is renovating a fixer-upper. (Every house is a fixer-upper.) Because he looks way too young to be retired, I ask him how old he is. "Sixty-seven," he says and I am completely shocked. "I hike a lot," he says. Across the street is the town coffee shop and internet café, Carrizozo Joe's. We each order a coffee. Over my objections, Ray pays for us both, and we sit on the deck under a not yet broiling sun. Ray would be a good friend if he lived on my block back home. He would be a good friend if I moved out here. After an hour of talking about life in the Tularosa Basin, our kids and when to take social security, Ray spots a large man with lion's mane hair, wearing shorts and a tie-dyed shirt, riding a beat-up girl's bike. "Sully," Ray shouts. Sully peddles over and sits with us. "Rick's out here from, where again?"

"Springfield, Massachusetts."

"You know Danny Walsh?" Sully says.

And here we go again. I don't know Danny Walsh, but I know his wife Kateri. She's on the Springfield City Council and was a student of mine twenty years ago. Sully and Danny grew up together in New York City and did two tours of duty, side by side, in Vietnam. "He's my best friend," Sully says. I take a bunch of pictures, and will show them to Kateri and Danny when I get home. Carrizozo is growing on me.

The Carrizozo Malpais is just west of town. At Valley of the Fires Recreation Area, a camping and nature site next to the fifteen-hundred-year-old, forty-mile-long lava flow, is a small hill with a few fixed large binoculars and a map on a concrete slab. About a dozen miles southwest of here is Trinity Site, where the world's first Atomic Bomb was detonated. I ask an old man, a tour guide, about that day.

"Were you here? Did the radiation hit Carrizozo?"

He chuckles as he says, "Sun come up twice that day. Wind from the west, so most likely we got dusted." Then he points north, "See that cone out on the Malpais? That blip? Before the bomb, when I was fourteen, my friends and me, got a bunch of old tires and hauled 'em up to that spot and lit 'em. Back in town everyone swore the volcano was erupting again. Scared 'em as bad as the bomb did. My father whacked me good."

I am loving this place. I want to hike with Nick on trails through the lava. I want to show him Trinity Site.

Over the next few days I meet a bunch of artists who've taken over part of the town. There are potters, painters, woodworkers, craftspersons, photographers, sculptors, and cartoonists. Most of 12th street is being rehabbed, battered-building by battered-building, into a much less expensive, less ambitious Taos. And best of all, I'm here in time for something called The Parade of the Burros, an annual event where artists paint life-sized plastic donkeys all sorts of crazy beautiful colors and designs. Tonight there's an art show in one of the fixed-up places, Gallery 408. And in the sculpture courtyard between that building and Gallery 412, next door, a guy who used to play backup for John Denver sings and strums, and people drink wine, and laugh in the warm night air under a starry sky; I want to start looking for property.

For two plus weeks I've lived in the motel. Every morning, after I call Nick, who still isn't talking much, I hang out with my new friends, Ray, Sully, Sheila and Ivy and all the artists. No one I meet seems angry or bitter, no one bitches or moans. Well, except for the guy who co-owns the motel where I'm staying. He thinks every man caught crossing the border without papers ought to have exploding microchips sewn into his scrotum so if he tries to cross again, the guy's nuts'll be blown off. He laughs and then seems disappointed when I don't laugh with him. I like him less than the rattlesnake that lunged at my leg when I was taking pictures alongside the railroad tracks.

The Saturday night before I leave for Las Vegas, a going-away-hope-you-come-back party is given in my honor. Everyone brings a dish. I bring wines from a local vineyard down the road in Tularosa. Sully offers to sell me his house, Ray says he'll help me renovate it, and I'm having a hard time not staring at the town's artist-in-residence, a beautiful woman from Germany. I'm sold on this place. I want Nick to like it, too. I cannot wait to show him.

Two days later I see Nick walking down the ramp at the airport. He's dressed in his yellow and black Ultimate Frisbee team shirt; the traffic sign for "Slow Children" is on the front, number 6 for Celtics legend Bill Russell is on the back. He has a Red Sox World Series '04 cap on his head. His face is bruised and puffy around one eye. I grab him and give him a hug. I'm met with the same deadweight I used to give my father.

"Good trip?" I ask.

"Not bad," he says. Then awkward silence.

"Just missed Dave Cowens," I say, hoping we can start a conversation about the Hall of Fame Celtic who walked through the airport a couple of minutes ago.

"Oh," he mutters.

"Very tall," I say.

"Yup."

We get Nick's bag and head out for a 2AM breakfast at a casino, then off to the hotel I'd checked into earlier in the day. We grunt a conversation about the trip, the food, the weather, the room. He won't talk about the beating or his arrest. Nick says he's very tired.

In the morning, our eyes widen as we drive through Zion National Park. Nick grabs the camera from my bag and takes many pictures. "Look at that," he says frequently. I'm grinning.

We swing through Kanab, Utah, and once again I tell Nick about the trip I took last year when I interviewed a woman who changed her life in mid-life. She made big money in New York City, but gave it up to follow her heart—rescuing greyhounds, three dozen at a time, out here where the bagels are lousy, and the pace of life is perfect. I wanted to know how she did it. I wanted to know the secret. Her mystical answer was, "Just do what you like." She was right.

Then it's south on Route 89 into Arizona and the wide-open sky. We take it all in and seem to be getting along. Nick naps now and then. When he snoozes, we drive in silence, my son asleep, me happy.

We spend the night in Gallup, New Mexico, get an early start in the morning, and by lunchtime we pull into Carrizozo. I show him the town—the 12th street art studios, the Chamber of Commerce caboose, the Malpais. I introduce him to the people I have talked about almost nonstop since we left Las Vegas. Nick is not rude to anyone, because he is not a rude kid, but he is not impressed by any of this—not the town, not the terrain, not the friends I've made. I can see it on his face. It seems to say, "All the way out here for this?" I want to take Nick to White Oaks to visit Ivy.

He grumbles, "Let's just get on the road."

But I have the keys. "Get in," I say.

And surprise! Nick likes Ivy. Of the new friends I've made she is by far the one he likes best. Maybe it's because she lives in the middle of nowhere in a house she built with her bare hands, or that she greets us with a big smile, or throws a mean Frisbee, or that she talks with Nick and laughs at the funny things he says. I buy a few pieces of her work, we three take pictures, share some hugs, promise to stay in touch, and Nick and I reluctantly leave.

We stop at the No Scum on our way out. I want to buy Nick a beer. Nick is two years away from drinking legally, but he has his nineteen-year-old cousin's fake ID. In real life John-Henry doesn't look like Nick, but the bartender okays the blurred New York driver's license and sets up a Budweiser for each of us, that, because of the near 7000-foot altitude, knocks Nick on his ass. He likes this place a lot; the busty-mannequin-tip-jar, the license plates, the full-sized Billy the Kid portrait, but he is most intrigued by the hundreds of dollar bills on the ceiling. "Can I have a dollar?" Nick gets a marker from the bar and writes, "Sebastian Telfair, best point guard in the NBA." And of course, he and I argue. I don't give a shit about Sebastian Telfair, but he's dead wrong. Telfair is an overrated kid out of New York who isn't nearly as good as another new point guard named Rajon Rondo. Why do Nick and I argue about two rookie point guards for a lousy Boston Celtic team? Because that's what we do.

We start our long ride home; south on Route 54, back through Carrizozo, and then past a nothing town, Oscuro, where at the end of a dirt road a locked gate keeps people away from where the first Atomic Bomb was detonated. We drive through Tularosa, and Alamogordo, and White Sands, and on to El Paso where we pick up Interstate 10 and head east. My son is aching to drive, and I relent. Nick takes the wheel.

I get a piercing stare thrown at me when I see a truck swerve. I say, "Look out."

"You don't trust me, do you?"

I fumble for an answer. "No, it's just that I'm not used to being the passenger."

"Sure. Right."

An hour past El Paso, to the north and west of us, the sun has been blocked by clouds that have risen to the moon; red, orange and maroon streaks bleed from the sky. The storm is a monster— tall, wide, and consuming. I can't take my eyes off it. I feel the wind pick up. I want the wheel back in my hands.

"You tired?" I ask.

"No," he mumbles.

"Maybe you want to switch for a while?"

And it begins. I'm told for the next five hundred miles that I'm an asshole of a father who has never trusted him, who has never really cared about him.

"What? I love you."

"All you ever do is yell at me." His list is long. I listen. I ache. I don't fight back.

In my head, I make my own list: All the times I ignored him. All the times I got angry at him for not liking the things I liked, for not being the way I wanted him to be, for not being like me. All the times I got screaming mad at him when I was really screaming mad at his mother in this never-ending tug-o-war. She takes multiple yearly trips to Disneyworld, and he comes home a Mouseketeer. I get box seats to see the Sox and Orioles at Camden Yards, and he wants to go back to the hotel and watch cartoons. God, I hate that Disney was even born.

All of this makes me think of me and my father and the distance we kept, the pain we caused each other: That I never bothered to understand him; an orphaned eight-year-old in the Depression, raised by people who, at best, tolerated him, whose only way out was World War Two. Hell, I wouldn't even let him come to my baseball games when I was in high school. And I think of the painful things he did to me; highest on the list, not telling my over-worried, controlling, crazy mother to leave the kid alone. How I hoped that my dad loved me, that he liked me. And now, dammit, here we are in another generational circle. My son wants to know that his father likes, and loves him, too. I don't want to wait until the end the way my father and I have. I don't want to be sick and old and dying, and finally have my son know in his bones that I love him, and like him, and am proud of him. I apologize to Nick, but Nick isn't ready.

Nick's been driving for hours. It's dark, and the wind is mad but the storm will pass while we sleep at a cheap motel in Odessa. The next morning is quiet and still. I drive some, Nick drives some, we talk, but not much. Outside of Longview, Nick notices that we're near Shreveport, Louisiana, where the mother of a friend of his now lives with her husband. Nick texts the kid, gets his mother's number, and gives her a call to say hi.

Karen, the kid's mom, wants us to stop by, and in an hour we're inside a gated community, sitting in a richly decorated McMansion, waiting for her husband Chris, a colonel, to come home from a round of golf at Barksdale Air Force Base. A few years ago, Chris helped me learn how to play golf when he was stationed at Westover Air Force base in Chicopee (home of the Vogels so I recently learned). I like Chris, but other than golf and a few nights of poker, we've never spent much of time together. Nick, on the other hand, has spent a lot of time with Karen and Chris at their house when they lived back in Massachusetts. They like Nick very much. I never met a parent who didn't.

After supper, the four of us head to Barksdale to see the country-rock musician, Charlie Daniels, do an outdoor show for the troops. He's tall and round and wears an American flag shirt with a hubcap-sized belt buckle over his giant belly. The brim on his ten-gallon hat is the size of an extra-large pizza. Charlie plays fiddle loud and strong and sings with a southern twang that's perfect. The crowd loves him. We do, too.

Nick and I sit up front in the VIP section with generals and colonels. A few thousand enlisted people are far behind us. I'm aware that Nick and I are dressed in sweaty shorts, tee shirts, and sandals. The generals and colonels aren't in uniform, but they're all crisp and clean. Charlie does his VERY patriotic songs, punctuated by unbelievably right wing rants. The officers smile and clap, and a few whistle loud through their teeth. I turn to Chris and ask, "Are Nick and I the only Democrats here?" Chris looks around, pauses, and says, "Pretty much." But what the hell, the guy can play, the night is warm, and the bugs aren't too fierce.

Then Charlie really grabs the crowd. He sings his two most popular songs, "The South's Gonna Do It Again," and "The Devil Went Down to Georgia." Possibly because he has run out of all the flag-waving things he could think of to whip up the crowd more than it already is, he growls into the microphone, "I don't care what anybody says (... pause for effect ...) I'm against child molesters." The crowd goes nuts.

"And who exactly is *for* child molesters?" Nick asks. And for the first time in a long time, we look at each other, and laugh and giggle together in a milk-runs-out-of-your-nose moment.

The next morning we leave for New Orleans and drive through what's left of the city, not quite a year after Katrina almost washed it away. I will always remember the smell.

We eat lunch at the Acme Oyster Bar. I have many oysters, Nick has Jambalaya. I tell him stories about being in New Orleans at American Psychological Association convention with his grandfather seventeen years ago. I'm smiling as I tell Nick about the Hurricanes we drank, the old friends his grandfather saw, and the night a former student of his got a huge national award. In front of a large crowd, the honoree mentioned three people who made a difference in his life; two were very famous psychologists, and then there was, "Henry Paar, you probably don't know him, but I learned more from him than anybody." And just as his former student was saying this, by coincidence, a camera crew was videotaping our row. That night we saw ourselves on the TV news, sniffing back happy tears. Nicky can't stop smiling. He loves Pop more than anyone else in the world.

We leave New Orleans on highway 90 and head through Mississippi. The coast is beaten; boats are landlocked, houses and businesses are torn and broken and aren't even boarded up. Nick and I look at each other and then out the window to the misery the storm has left. We stay on highway 90 until we can go no farther; the bridge over Bay St. Louis is washed away. We go back over the road that got us here and figure out another way home.

***

It's a little over two years after our trip. My father is dying. Everyone in the family is with him: my mother and sister Robyn, Nick and Chelsea, my nephews Ethan and John-Henry, my brother-in-law John. Each person has had a private moment with him to say what needs to be said. He's not responding; he probably can't hear by now. There's a pause just before his lungs rumble, then his lips move as if he were talking to someone. His head reaches up a small fraction ... and he stops breathing. It's over and I cannot tell that he has died. At the immediate end, there is so little difference between life and death. We all cry and hold each other as we clear the room and gather in the hall.

I go back in the room to spend time alone with my dad. I sit in a chair on his left and hold his still warm hand. I tell him that I'm glad he was my father, that I'm happy he and I finished our hurt before he left, that I'm sorry I didn't really understand him until the last few years of his life. That I loved him dearly. That I always will.

Nick joins us. He sits in a chair on his grandfather's right and holds his hand too. I tell him that I know Pop was his favorite person in the world, just as my grandfather was mine. I reach for Nick's right hand with my left and we make a circle. Nick tells me he loves me. My eyes blur. I apologize to him for being an asshole. He says he loves me anyway.

Acknowledgements

Thank you to Chelsea and Nick. I love you both. Every day I thank the universe that you two kind, generous, and loving people are my children.

Thank you to Straw Dog Writers' Guild and its members. You have been warm and welcoming to those of us wrestling with words.

Great thanks to The Garage Band: Jacqueline Sheehan, Ed Orzechowski, Jovonna Van Pelt, Stephanie Shafran, and Beth Filson. We have the COVID lockdown to thank for us getting together, sharing our work, and encouraging each other to keep writing no matter what.

Thanks to Claudia Presto who kicked over the table, quit her job, and moved to Kanab, Utah to do what she wanted to do, which was rescuing greyhounds.

And finally, thank you to Elizabeth MacDuffie and Mark Miller for your great support of writers in Western Massachusetts, and for wanting to publish my story.

About the author:

Rick Paar is a psychologist who writes novels, short stories, and essays. He lives in Western Massachusetts, has two grown children, Nick and Chelsea, and a grandson, Wyatt.